Ah, Those
Irish Colleens!

Published by
   Cumberland House Publishing, Inc.
   431 Harding Industrial Drive
   Nashville, TN 37211

Cover design: Unlikely Suburban Design
Text design: Lisa Taylor
Illustrations: Michael Allen Lowe

Library of Congress Cataloging-in-Publication Data
Folsom, Helen Walsh.
   Ah, those Irish colleens! : heroic women of Ireland / by Helen
Walsh Folsom ; illustrated by Michael Allen Lowe.
      p. cm.
Includes index.
   ISBN 1-58182-355-X (pbk.)
1. Women—Ireland—Biography. 2. Ireland—Biography. I. Title.
   CT3650.I73F65 2003
   920.72'09415—dc22

                                                          2003019676

Printed in the United States of America
1 2 3 4 5 6 7 8 — 08 07 06 05 04 03

Ah, Those Irish Colleens!

Heroic Women of Ireland

Helen Walsh Folsom

Illustrated by
Michael Allen Lowe

CUMERLAND HOUSE
NASHVILLE, TENNESSEE

Thank you to the Lord God of Words, who set us apart from the animals and made us just a little lower than the angels. And thank you to my wonderful children, Bill, Belinda, Butch, and Bettse, for their loving encouragement.

Acknowledgments

"No Irish need apply" was a statement attached to "Help Wanted" placards in mid-nineteenth-century America. However, by 1940, America was obsessed with Irish-mania. Playwrights, authors, actors, singers, songwriters filled the media with Irish charm. Given my Irish heritage, how could I not be caught up in pride?

No wonder then, when I decided to write full time, I chose a subject I could never grow tired of—Ireland. The delightful mystery and warmth of the Irish people and the strange attraction of the misty bogs and mountains of the green land captivate the imagination with nostalgia, even if you have never been there.

There were 250,000 Irish in America before the American Revolution. Irish generals, admirals, and the perpetual Irish Brigade were major factors in our victory. After the war, Lord Mountjoy stood up before the British Parliament and declared, "We have lost America to the Irish!"

They had indeed. The Irish have captured America's heart.

Many people have touched me personally to help me present things Irish:

My Irish great-grandmother, Lizzie Walsh Smith, whose family fled the Famine and came to America, the "Land of Tír na nÓg," in 1849.

Charles Perdue, Director of Wyandotte County

Libraries, a fellow lover of the Ould Sod, for his encouragement.

Publisher Ron Pitkin at Cumberland House for his interest in fascinating Irish "colleens."

My daughter Bettse for her faith in me.

Contents

Introduction

Deep in the mists and dark green forests of the land of Eirinn, long before the Roman Empire spread its greedy fingers across the Western world, the Celts lived according to a table of democratic regulations called the Brehon laws. The Brehons were indeed so democratic that the rights of women were equal to those of men. Women had the right to own property, rule territories, sue for divorce, and go physically into battle. The awesome Irish champion, Cuchulain, whose statue now adorns the lobby of the General Post Office in Dublin, was the greatest warrior of all time, and he learned his fighting skills from Scathach, a woman warrior.

Now then, after some recent centuries of contention over women's rights, it seems that women everywhere are once again claiming their prerogatives. What gentlemen don't know, and women have always known, is that the female has always ruled the world. Oh, it's been a subtle control; a word of flattery here, a tantrum there, a bit of coaxing and the promise of certain relative delights on occasion—and milady will have her way. Sometimes they brought about disaster, sometimes victory, often blunders, but always an impact of some kind on their peers.

Let me welcome you into the world of women in Ireland: Queen Maeve, Grace O'Malley, Red Mary, Speranza, Kitty O'Shea, and more of the colleens whose love, fury, greed, patriotism—a multitude of motives and emotions—moved governments and heroes and aesthetics and changed Irish history.

Ah, Those
Irish Colleens!

Queen Maeve, the Warrior Queen

It was about the time of Christ. Roman armies ruled the world, but did not quite make it across the Irish Sea to the lush, green land of Eirinn before the Roman Empire began to shake and crumble. And so, Ireland remained a country of ancient traditions and many small kingships. Divided into four provinces, Ulster, Munster, Leinster and Connaught, the kings gained respect, and many exaggerated powers by force. Every three years, all the kings of the land gathered at the Hill of Tara to elect the new Ard Ri, high king of the whole island.

Maeve, ex-wife of the powerful Conovar MacNessa, king of the northern province of Ulster, inherited the monarchy of her father, Feiloch, and became queen of Connaught, the western province. Many legends have been told of her valiant wars, the most popular in-

cident being the Tain bo Cuailgne, the Cattle Raid of Cooley.

In 1765, one James McPherson, a writer, claimed to put together all the stories in his epic work, The Ossian Tales. *Taking only the barest fragments and weaving them together with fabricated magic and witchcraft, he produced a brand-new myth, which has been accepted as authentic by some over the past two centuries.*

The true story of the adventure, discovered while exploring ancient annals, is rich with excitement and action.

The burly, brindled horse stood very still in his traces; the wagon moved not an inch. With confidence, Maeve lifted herself to stand tall in her war chariot, raised her spear, and narrowed her blue eyes to judge the distance to the wicker dummy on the far side of the lea. She hefted the shaft of the lance once. Suddenly her powerful arm shot forward, and the spear flew across the field and embedded, quivering, in the heart of the straw man.

Around Maeve, her warriors shouted praises.

"The heaviest spear ever made!"

"The target so far and her lance so sure!"

"Queen Maeve is yet the grandest warrior on the field!"

Maeve, though gratified by the praise, was not yet satisfied. She sent for her spear and prepared to practice time after time until she was sure that the success of her throw was not a lucky chance, but a certainty.

Chill, wet gales from the ocean thrilled her well-trained body with energy. Dark blue clouds rolled slowly over the mountaintops and dampened her woolen cloak and loose, linen dress. She pushed the folds of the plaid cloak back over her shoulders so that her smooth arms were free to cast the spear. Soft raindrops wet her cheeks and soaked her heavy, black hair and refreshed her vigor as she trained.

Strong as she was, forceful as was her nature, there was a spot inside her breast that appreciated the exquisite beauty of rainbows against the dark eastern sky as the showers passed on over rich green oak trees. She loved her land, Eire, the lush island in the wild sea.

Tenderness aroused by the natural loveliness of the countryside reminded her of her good husband, Oilioll. Gentle, he was, no fighter, but it was that fact that made him the perfect foil for Maeve's wild, aggressive spirit. It was seldom that he disagreed with her decisions or advanced an i of which she might not approve. She was, after all, the queen of Connaught, the western side of Eire, with its stony mountains and breathtaking sea and skyscapes.

But she respected the dear fellow in spite of his timid ways. He was a lively lover and had given her seven fine sons, the Seven Maines, the villagers called them, and a pretty daughter, Finnabair. The oldest boy was now twenty years plus, and the youngest just ready to practice with a sword.

Daylight waned, and Maeve led her warriors home from their war games to the settlement around her palace at Cruachan. It was dusk when her chariot clanged over the earthen ramparts into the courtyard surrounded by pales. Just before she passed through the carved, wooden pillars at the gate, she caught sight of a cluster of people rising to their feet to salute her.

Who could they be? Pitiful they were, more ragged than most of her subjects, in faded, worn cloaks and shabby, woollen trousers. Odd-looking, too. Not as tall as most Celts, and their skin was tanner. She nodded at them as she drove her big horse on by.

Torches gave light inside the great hall of Cruachan. It was a huge, oaken mansion her father had built in honor of her mother. The outer walls of the round building were made of standing oak logs with fine carvings of the gods. Inside, the rooms were divided by smooth panels hung with rich furs and decorated with golden shields; the grand hall where they ate and held court was the most elaborate of them all. Maeve's leather sandals slapped the stone flags on the floor as she strode into the room.

Unpinning the large, golden brooch that held her cloak onto her shoulders, she let the garment fall to the floor. Then she dropped onto the large bench beside a heavy trestle table and reached for a shank of roasted venison waiting for her on a platter. Just before she sank her white teeth into the hot, juicy meat, Oilioll appeared.

Maeve frowned. He looked agitated. Under his heavy cloak she saw his hands rubbing together nervously.

"Well then, my king, what are you troubled about, and would it have anything to do with that ragged mob outside the gates?"

"It does."

With her mouth full, Maeve mumbled, "Tell me."

"At your wish, I will ask them to come in and they may ask you themselves."

"Call them now, unless you think they are starved and will kill me for their dinner."

Oilioll's narrow face broke into a smile. "I have already fed the wretches," he said as he left the house through the high door-gates.

In they shuffled, about twenty of them, and clustered in front of Maeve. They looked weary and sad, but their heads were held high and the spokesman made no apology for their appearance or their boldness.

"Queen Maeve," he began. "We are Firbolgs, a lost people. Many centuries ago, this island belonged to our race. Then came the de Danaans and pushed us into a corner here in Connaught. Finally, we had to leave when your Milesians came and forced us out altogether. We have lived in Albany among the Picts and Scots for many long years.

"Now then, Roman rulers have put upon us burdens we could not bear, so we left that island and came to Eire. The king of Leinster in the east, Cairbre is his name, allowed us to settle on his lands in the east, but he has exacted from us terrible rents to fill his barns and keep him wealthy.

"King Oilioll, you being a man of our race, we beg from you and your queen lands of our own where we may live in peace and prosper, as befits a noble race of people. We will pledge loyalty to your crown in peace and war, if you will only give us a place to settle."

Oilioll stroked his dark beard. Himself a descendant of the Firbolgs, one of the few clans that hid in the hills and managed to remain in Eire, he understood their desperation.

But Maeve was the true sovereign of Connaught. The daughter of Eochid Feiloch, once the high king of Ireland, Maeve was given in marriage to Conovar MacNessa, king of Ulster in the north. It was a poor match. He couldn't bear her insolent, aggressive spirit, and she defied his domineering attempts to control her. It was no surprise to her when, on a cold, wet first day of February, he confronted her and loudly stated, "I divorce you!"

"Praise be to Brigid, the wise goddess whose feast day makes it possible for me to leave you, pompous pig that you are! If you had not declared our marriage done, I would have said it myself!" was Maeve's arrogant response. Inwardly, she writhed with fury, for she would have preferred to be first to declare him an unfit husband and be free of him. Now it would appear that he had discarded *her*, and the stigma would follow her throughout her lifetime.

Angrily, she gathered up the things she had brought into the marriage, cattle and horses, golden bowls and brooches, her own sword and battle axe, and several fine wolfskin robes, and she set out to live in her father's territory in Connaught. After King Eochid's death, she claimed the rule of his kingship, and no one seemed inclined to argue with the fiery, militant woman.

Conovar didn't marry again for a while. He hinted that he was biding his time for a prize worthy of his grand self. Finally, after a disappointment of seven years, he married Maeve's spiritless sister, Ethne.

Oilioll was Maeve's second husband, a man of peace. He could not complain about his wife. In her own way, she was all he could want. He had no wish to make heavy decisions or control the country, and as far as his kingly powers went, it would be totally up to the rambunctious queen whether or not they would help this poor, displaced tribe trying to escape from tyranny.

Certainly, there was open land in the west of the island, if you wanted to call it land. Mountains and plateaus made of loose, gray stones filled most of the space. Great slabs of stone outcroppings projected from embankments, proving that there was unyielding rock under every precious hill of grass.

"So, you think you have a right to land in Eire?" she asked.

"We do." The answer was definite, unwavering. Maeve liked that.

"And have you appealed to the Red Branch Knights of Ulster? Their duty is to enforce the Brehon laws and give justice to all people, rich or poor."

"We have. King Conovar MacNessa scorned us. He said we are intruders whose rights are long lost in the passing of time. He said there was no place in Eire for Firbolgs."

"Indeed. He said that, did he? Conovar MacNessa said that?" Maeve stood up, majestically gesturing with her arm raised high. "Conovar is an arrogant, selfish fool. He has enough cattle in his herd to feed the entire island. His lands spread all across the north, and there is plenty of space for settlers in Ulster, even if he doesn't want to antagonize Cairbre. So he turned you down; he ordered the Red Branch Knights to ignore your rights. So be it. We will make room and enough for your people in Connaught. My only demand from you is that you will swear loyalty to me, fight my battles, and obey my commands."

"That we will, Queen Maeve."

Hesitantly, Oilioll murmured, "And what if Cairbre becomes angry with you for taking away his laborers, my love?"

A smile of disdain crossed the face of the warrior queen. "It would give me great pleasure to meet him in battle and try my skills with sword and spear!"

It wasn't long before Oilioll was pleased to see the displaced tribe move like a tide from the eastern province into the rough, stony hills of Connaught. They made themselves stone huts. They fished in the crystal lakes and streams. They scratched out fields for grain and meadows between the huge, gray stone hills and on the green, grassy slopes east of the Burren. With them when they came were a few straggling cattle, but not enough to give the people all of the milk, butter, and leather they could have used. Maeve rode her chariot through the hills, over high areas where she could see the beautiful lakes lying like mirrors of the sky in the distance. Huts dotted the green areas and hearth smoke blew eastward, chased by the Atlantic gales. She was satisfied that she had for herself thousands of new subjects who would fight her battles and support her wealth.

But something kept eating at her thoughts. All those

magnificent herds of cattle grazing fat in the green fields of Ulster in Conovar MacNessa's north country. The Firbolgs could use some of that bounty. Truthfully, she didn't particularly covet them for the Firbolgs, but it irked her that the man who repulsed her as his wife should have so much good.

He was commander of the Red Branch Knights, the most highly trained, elite soldiery anywhere. No one dared infringe on Conovar's lands or property with the Knights on guard. A new champion had recently appeared and joined their ranks, a lad named Cuchulain, supposed to be the best fighter in all of Ireland, invincible.

"We are going to raid the cattle herd of Conovar MacNessa," she told Oilioll one day. "Your Firbolgs are in need of livestock in order to survive. Conovar has more than he needs. He deserves to provide for them since he was spiteful and denied them protection."

"Maeve, my dear love, you must not be impulsive about this. It would take a great army to challenge Conovar's Red Branch Knights. Our own herds will grow, and we can provide cows and a bull now and then to the farmers."

"It would take too many years to do that. I have heard there is the finest bull in all of Eire in Conovar's herd. That bull will sire many a healthy calf, and the herds of Connaught will blossom like the Maybush!"

Maeve stood tall and faced her husband. He was a good enough fellow. She was proud of the Princes of Maines and her princess. But the man was timid, very reluctant to instigate any kind of conflict with the other kings. Maeve had no such qualms. Fighting among the many kings of the island was a way of life, and had been for long centuries, since the time of the only supreme ruler of Eire, Queen Macha.

No matter. She would leave him at home to keep order while she led an army into Ulster and brought back enough cattle to spread across Connaught and bring wealth and splendor to her kingdom.

And Conovar MacNessa, her sister's husband, the man who dared to despise Maeve ni Feiloch, would learn a lesson, she thought with arrogant satisfaction.

Couriers rode out across the countryside. Queen Maeve was building an army, a grand squad of men who would sweep into Ulster and bring back many head of fine cattle to seed the poor farmers' homesteads and provide hearty food for their families. Praise the queen who took care of her subjects!

Before long, thousands of men were prepared, with spears and swords, battle axes and shields, to fight for Maeve. As many as possible were provided with horses and taught to ride and fight, while valiant Maeve rode among them in her war chariot, shouting commands. They were ready to go north to raid the wealth of Ulster, and particularly in Maeve's mind, to prick the bloated conceit of Conovar MacNessa.

The champions she chose to lead her army were Keat MacMagach and Fergus MacRoigh. Fergus had come to Connaught a few years before, bringing his army of three thousand warriors. He nursed a healthy hate for his uncle Conovar.

"The man is as evil as the Bel himself," Fergus growled, running his hand through the thick, red waves of his hair. "Because of his powerful army, he forced me out of my rightful place on the throne of Ulster after my father died. He has not a splinter of truth in his tongue nor a wren's yolk of mercy in his heart. He used my reputation to lure the sons of Uisnach into an ambush and tricked me into staying behind and sending my sons to protect them. Determined to retaliate for being humiliated and spurned, he lied and schemed, and his treachery brought about the vicious murder of my sons. Gladly I will go with you to slice away at his wealth and pride! I want to have the chance to face him and take his life's blood!" He slammed his axe against a near oak tree and brought down a rain of leaves.

Through the bogs and lakelets of Erne, Maeve's army trooped to the grassy plain of Cuailagne near Slieve Gullian. She led them standing in her chariot, a robe of white wolfskin slung over her shoulders, a golden circlet crowning her dark hair, which had been drawn into a rich braid to keep it out of the way of her sword arm. Among the warriors, rode five of the Seven Maines, grand fighters all, taking joy in the opportunity to help their Queen Mother lead into battle.

With skill, the riders surrounded a huge herd of Ulster cattle and turned them westward toward Connaught. Her foot soldiers made short work of the squad of servants who had been watching the livestock, all but a few who took off for the palace of Emania, where Conovar lived in smug majesty.

"Conovar will be sending the Red Branch right on our heels," Fergus told Maeve. "Prepare to defend, my lady."

"I will do more than that." Maeve smiled. "Keat!" she called her other champion to come on his horse to the side of her chariot.

As he rode close, she shouted, "Keat, I want you to take half of the troops and drive the herd to Connaught. I have other work for Fergus and our half of the army."

Swiftly the thousands of warriors were divided, and Keat moved the herd westward.

"Bring your army with me," Maeve told Fergus. "We have a little work to do at Emania."

"So we will!" the delighted man shouted. "The Red Branch will be chasing the cattle, and we will take Conovar and Emania. I hope I find Conovar there."

They traveled hard for days, but by the time they reached the capital of Emania, Conovar was not there. They learned that the Knights had indeed rushed off after the cattle herd with King Conovar at their head. Nor were the family nor the servants of Emania still in the fort, having scattered in fear.

"No matter," Maeve exulted. "He will have little left after we finish here."

They set to work stripping the palace of golden utensils, jewelry of the king and queen and rich sets of clothing left behind in their hurry to depart. They tore down the heavy, wooden walls of the Great Hall, where Conovar often entertained other kings, and they set fire to the remains. Finding the armory where the Red Branch Knights kept their weapons and booty, they carried off all of the pieces that had been left.

From a smaller building, clearly an infirmary, came crippled and maimed knights, struggling to fight off the intruders as best they could in their battle-wounded state. Maeve scorned to fight the brave, old soldiers and chased them back inside their shelter.

Then she and Fergus turned their happy raiders toward home.

It was rather slow-going with all their plunder to carry. Some of the booty was loaded onto confiscated carts and wagons, but they were awkward, trundling over the stony land. Finally, as they neared the River Breffney, they came upon the remains of a terrible battle. Bodies were strewn over the grass, and the earth was covered with blood. And there, along with his brave men, lay Keat MacMagach.

"It was Conall Kearnach and the Red Branch," a fallen Firbolg struggled to tell Maeve and Fergus. "Keat was valiant. He slung a brain-ball at King Conovar, and it struck him in the head. The king was knocked off his horse, but seemed to still live. Conall had with him young Cuchulain. We were no match for them. They sent the cattle back."

"And which way did the army leave?"

"Yon there." The poor man pointed before he breathed his last. His finger directed them to the west, toward Cruachan and the queen's palace.

"Oilioll!" Maeve whipped her horses and rode furiously over the hills. Her horse warriors were close behind, and the foot soldiers drove wagons and carried their booty running after them.

It took too much time to reach the capital village. Smoke rose behind the stone walls that sheltered the palace and drifted out the darkened, open doorway. Maeve's horses hurdled the ramparts and raced across the bridge. She leaped from the cart to run to the building.

Inside, it was clear that Conall's forces were bent on destroying all that belonged to Maeve. Everything was torn, burnt, or gone entirely.

But the horror of it all was, just inside the outer doors, King Oilioll lay, a large, heavy spear still embedded in his chest. Conovar must have despised Oilioll for his timidity, for the little king's head was still attached to his shoulders instead of riding next to the Ulster king's knee on his saddle.

From Maeve's throat came a most awful cry. It was not a wail of grief only, but an almost animal battle cry of rage! Her man was dead. Her king. His gentle heart was pierced, and his blood spread across the stone flags.

Beside her, Fergus MacRoigh spoke in a cold, mechanical murmur. "Thus so was my son's body pierced, lying in the mud of a rampart. And thus would I have cried out if I could speak at all. I have no comfort for you, lady."

Maeve screamed for her men. When they came, she ordered them to place the king's body on a bier and cover it with badger skins and protect it for burial in a proper royal cairn when she returned.

"And your sons, Queen Maeve?"

"My sons?"

"One lies in the water of the stream outside, his sword still in his young hand. The other, the smaller, we found hanged in the burning loft above here."

"Their brothers will avenge them when we find Conall," her low voice trembled, tight, fighting for control.

It took a long time to follow Conall Kearnach and the Knights across Eire. Her men were bone weary and had to rest, as did their horses. Through the long nights, while they slept, she walked the ridges in an agonized watch. She beat her breast. She tore at her black hair. That terrible cry welled up in her throat and had to be stifled until she choked on it.

Fergus sat by the night fire watching the queen in her agony. He would not attempt to calm or comfort her. She needed these nights while fury and pain warred in her heart along with self-chastisement for leaving her good husband to the savage vengeance of Conovar and his champion, Conall. Maeve was going to need all her hate and ferocity built to a white heat when they found the army of Ulster.

As for Fergus, he had long since mastered his hate. It sat in his heart like molten rock, solid, entrenched, ready to take revenge when the time came.

But Conall's men were slowly herding the cattle back home, confident that the spiteful attacks of Maeve's army were properly rebuffed. At last her spies returned to tell her that the Ulster army was camped for the night at the River Breffney, not far north of the site of the previous carnage of the Connaught raiders. Most of the Knights seemed to have gone to see to the castle at Emania. It would seem also that Conall, certain of his victory, was biding his time along with his herders.

Silently gathering the warriors together in the pale moonlight, Maeve left her noisy chariot behind and led her people on foot over the leas until they could see the fires of the encampment.

"I see Conall's standard there on the bank of the river." Her murmur was too deathly quiet, ominous. "I will go first. Wait for my call."

Like a cat, the Warrior Queen moved over the ground. They saw her reach a spot near the flag. Then they saw her dark silhouette in the firelight raise her sword and strike!

Instantly, that awful cry of rage came out of her and filled the air. The Connaught troops ran into the battle, the five Princes of Maines to the fore bent on revenge. The skeleton crew of soldiers, startled and dazed, nevertheless leaped to their feet. A battle ensued, a short carnage to be sure, but vicious and frantic. Men were slashed, speared, and crushed with heavy weapons. Maeve's young princes fell.

The Ulster warriors saw that they were outnumbered severely by the wild Connaughts, and Conall, their leader, lay dead, his head severed from his body by Maeve's single stroke. They ran for their horses and fled. The foot soldiers that herded the cattle scattered into the woods. The herd was Maeve's again. Slowly, the livestock was turned toward Cruachan.

"Conall's body there," Fergus called to Maeve. "Will you have his head?"

Maeve turned away. "He despised the head of my king. I despise him."

Travelling westward, Maeve rode sitting down in her chariot, depleted of fervor, weighted by sorrow.

"My men are weary," she said, driving her chariot along the banks of a river. "It has been a long time fighting for the cattle. Lives have been lost, even my children and my gracious Oilioll Mor. Conall Kearnach is dead by my hand. It is not enough. There is one more thing I must do. I want that grand bull of Ulster to sire fine cattle in Connaught. And I want the life of

Conovar MacNessa and Cuchulain, his champion. Surely, the blood of my king and my children cries for vengeance."

"There is only one who may be equal to Cuchulain's skills in combat." Fergus rubbed his red beard thoughtfully as he rode along beside the queen. "It's Firdia MacDamhain. He, too, is young and strong and well skilled. It's a Firbolg he is, of the Damnonian tribe, who have lived hidden in the mists of the islands of Irras Domhnan for centuries. Maeve, I have heard your brother, the bard Congal, sing of his exploits. He did not come forward to join your army, for the tribe is a strange, shy lot that keep to themselves."

"What will he take to challenge and kill Cuchulain? I will pay any price to kill the leader who so mercilessly murdered my husband and sons."

"And mine," Fergus reminded her. "Gold or cattle mean nothing to the Damnonians. But, I wonder . . . I have heard it said that the tribe is getting sickly because there is no new blood. Perhaps a wife? Better yet, a princess. Would you give your daughter, Finnabair, in marriage to him?"

"My daughter? Would she marry the one who takes vengeance for the death of her father? She will. Send for Firdia MacDamhain. Make the offer. If he refuses, I will slaughter his whole tribe!"

Maeve went back to Cruachan to wait for Firdia. She had work started on a huge cairn, a gravesite of monumental proportions, covered with stones, where she buried her gentle Oilioll Fionn Mor and her sons, the Seven Maines.

"Someday, I will rest beside them there," she said to

Fergus. "But not now. I have a quest to finish and a kingdom to rule."

Firdia appeared one day, quietly walking into the palace. Without fanfare he told Maeve he would do battle with Cuchulain of whom he had heard much.

"It will be a matter of interest to meet one so well known," he said with a puckish half grin.

Maeve studied the young man. He was slight of stature like so many of the Firbolgs, light on his feet. His short, dark hair was coarse and unruly, sticking out in all directions. He wore no beard. Most of the best fighters took care not to let their hair and beard get long, making it harder for their foes to grab hold and slash their throats.

But she wondered how he would handle Cuchulain, who she heard was very tall and thick of chest and arms. She asked Firdia.

"I will do it," he said calmly.

"Then let me put you to practice with some of our best warriors," she said.

Firdia MacDamhain turned his heel and started to leave.

"Where are you going?" Maeve demanded.

"I have no time nor strength to waste on play-acting at battle. Either I meet the grand Cuchulain and show my mettle or I go back to the bay where my people live in peace."

"Stay!" Maeve ordered. "It is a long way to the ford of Ardee, where they say Cuchulain resides, guarding the grand bull of Ulster. We should not be going all that way without assurance that you are the fighter they claim you are. But I will go. If you prove to be a liar, I will spread the lifeblood of your people all across Connaught. If you conquer the champion of Conovar MacNessa, I will pay you well."

"And the princess?"

"My daughter is a beautiful and honorable young woman. She will do as I say and marry you. I myself have borne seven fine sons, so she will serve well to increase your declining family."

On his tanned, pugnacious face, the impish smile spread again. A curious twinkle appeared in the bright, black eyes. "Let us be going then!"

A great part of Maeve's Connaught army came together again, many out of curiosity to see how such a wiry, little man planned to defeat the great hero of Eire.

The journey across the island took many days, days in which word traveled to every clachan and crannog of the challenge to Conovar's champion, and sure knowledge that, if indeed Firdia could kill Cuchulain, Maeve would claim the bull. A great crowd assembled at the River Murthaine. Red Branch Knights were there. They had heard of Firdia's unimpressive size and came to scoff and be certain there were no tricks.

The day came. Maeve's army camped on the western side of the Murthaine. Cuchulain stayed with the Knights in the woods on the east. A rough road led alongside the river on the eastern side until it came to a place of shallows where cattle had been driven and a man could easily walk across the ford of Ardee.

Cuchulain appeared from the woods. He was indeed tall, his tawny Celtic hair hanging rich and thick to his shoulders. Muscles like small mountains swelled from under his tunic.

Handsome, he was, and proud and daring.

In one hand he held a battle axe, in the other a long sword. He stopped and looked at the crowd on the other side of the stream, searching for Firdia MacDamhain, his challenger. No one came forward. He was puzzled.

Suddenly, from out of the crowd, leaped a wild, black sprite, screaming like a banshee! The creature flew forward, waving a razor-sharp knife only a foot long!

He shot into the stream, gave a lunge that plunged the knife into the hero's side, and danced backward out of reach, bloody blade still in his hand.

Instantly Cuchulain swung the axe in his direction and turned, slicing the air with the long sword. But the imp ducked and weaved under the big weapons and once more dug the knife into Cuchulain, this time in his thigh. The burning wounds only served to infuriate the Ulster champion. He threw down his axe and braced his feet in the water for the next assault. As the imp leaped behind the great man, Cuchulain thrust the sword point into Firdia's body, drawing blood from his back.

Without so much as a wince, Firdia charged again, clearly attempting to reach that massive chest with his knife. The sharp knife had only to reach some vital part, the heart or belly or throat; it was long enough to finish the battle at that and not heavy enough to slow down his prancing, taunting skills.

Time passed. The crowds roared on each side of the water, amazed and shocked that the great Cuchulain would find such an adversary in such a little man. The hero learned to protect his vitals from Firdia's swift lunges with the deadly dagger. Firdia kept moving, first here then there, dodging Cuchulain's sword, which could have sliced him in half if ever it met its mark.

Maeve stood in her chariot, staring at the amazing skill of her champion. Surely, a man worthy of her! The finest warrior in Eire!

Dark came on and in the twilight the watchers saw the swirl of battle continue. Torches were lit. Water flew as the warrior's limbs splashed and kicked, water mixed with blood.

Suddenly the scene stopped. A tangle of arms and legs and bodies lay in the middle of the stream. Silence. Who had won? Were they both dead? Had they killed each other?

Then something moved. Firdia. His head rose, then dropped aside as Cuchulain, the hero of Eire, pushed away the body of his enemy and stood up on unsteady legs. He trembled and nearly fell.

Then he bowed and, with his one good arm, lifted the body of Firdia MacDamhain from the water and raised it high over his head.

"Shout praises to the valiant hero of Connaught!" he cried. "The greatest fighter I have ever faced!"

Shouts went up! The Red Branch Knights rushed to help Cuchulain, bloody, slashed in many places but alive, to the shore. He brought the small body to the chariot of Maeve.

"Take your champion to his people. Bury him with honors in a fine cairn! Remember his name forever! He defended you well, Queen Maeve."

"I will."

"Indeed you will!" came a roar from across the stream. It was Conovar MacNessa himself, his curly, blonde beard and hair ragged and wild. Standing in his chariot above the crowd he waved his sword. "I challenge you, Maeve ni Feiloch! You who slept in my bed, unworthy of my favor! I challenge you, Fergus MacRoigh. You who lacks cleverness to defeat me. Come, one of you! Both of you! Let us do battle!"

Startled, Maeve and Fergus stared at Conovar. In the torchlight they saw that his head was misshapen, a black hole where his eye should be, a sunken place above it in his skull.

"The brain-ball thrown by Keat," Fergus said. "It has left him disfigured and mad. I, for one, would not demean myself to try to fight the devil. It would be a disgrace."

Maeve looked hard at the man waving his sword and ranting in the firelight. Slowly she raised her spear. Aiming the long, heavy shaft, she hefted it carefully. "I will not kill him," she said coldly. "He wants me to! He wants to die rather than live like that! I will not do him the honor."

Her spear shot forward across the stream, dashing toward the king. It seemed sure to take his head! Instead, it passed his raving face and sliced off the top of the torch that lighted it. Conovar MacNessa was left shouting into the dark, a madman begging to die.

It was over. Firdia MacDamhain was taken home to the Bay of Irras Domhnan, where his people mourned and celebrated him. The queen's sons were also honored. Each of them, from the eldest who died in battle to the youngest who defended their royal house, all had died valiantly.

Queen Maeve felt a surge of power and peace. Home she would go to restore the palace at Cruachan and guide her subjects, both Celts and Firbolgs, to years of prosperity. Yes, and battles, too.

〜⊘〜

Maeve did restore Cruachan, making the palace more grand and rich than ever. Her kingdom prospered with the addition of the hard-won cattle from Ulster.

Fergus MacRoigh became her third and last husband. They had three fine sons, Ciar, Corc, and Conmac. To Ciar, Maeve granted the land in the far southwest of Connaught, named after him to be Kerry.

She reigned over Connaught for a total of ninety-eight years, and was finally buried, standing up and facing the east, beside Oilioll Fionn Mor in the grand cairn which still rises at the top of Knockrea Mountain in County Sligo. She was one hundred and twenty years old.

Deirdre of the Sorrows

Traditionally, King Conovar MacNessa was a grand-looking man, powerful of build and handsome, with a curly, blonde beard; he was a strong ruler of his kingdom and a brilliant commander of his army, the Red Branch Knights. However, there was a dark side to the man. He was an unspeakable liar, trickster, and avaricious lecher when he was denied his wishes.

Cathbad the Druid stood before the open hearth in the dim, wood-walled room. His hood sagged over his face so that only his eyes glittered out of the black shadow, reflecting light from the flickering flames. In his hand he held a red, squirming and squalling infant, still wet from birthing. From the child's tiny, toothless mouth came screams of terror.

Slowly the priest raised his arm high, the coarse, brown sleeve of his robe falling back revealing a lean, white arm, the babe trembling in his hand, so that all of the men clustered in the room could see her.

"Bel, the great god of fire and darkness, has given to me a vision. A curse covers this woman-child. She will grow to great beauty, but she brings disaster to Eire. Three heroes of Ulster will die without the honor of battle. Seven years of shame will be the heritage of a king, and the eternal city of Emania Macha will be burned!"

Startled silence held the tongues of the men. They looked at the ugly, little, red thing fighting Cathbad's grip and imagined they could see death and disaster in her already.

King Conovar MacNessa himself, dressed in his royal white, red, and black cloak, a gigantic, golden brooch pinned at his massive breast, stood at the fire with a look of alarm in his piercing blue eyes. He had come to share the joy of the birth of the first child of his favorite bard, Feilimid. This threat of fate sent a thrill of alarm through his powerful body. Certainly, he must not allow any hint of fear to be seen by the nobles who had come with him, so he made his voice strong and it rang through the room.

"Tell me now, Cathbad," Conovar said to the Druid, "What must we do about this? How may we be rid of this curse?"

"With one snap of your thumb and finger, you could break her scrawny, little neck and be free of it all," Cathbad answered, still clinging with one hand to the writhing, squealing, wet and naked thing.

"Do it!"

"Destroy it quickly!"

"Kill the imp before her magic begins!"

The men welcomed with relief such a simple way to

overcome the curse. Life and death, child or man, was a moot situation with the Celts of Emania Macha. Lifeblood was spilled regularly, an accepted thing.

Tears coursed down into the bronze beard of the bard, the father of the tiny infant. Feilimid wanted to speak, to beg for the life of his child, the first and last of the woman who lay dead in the darkened room behind him. But how could he ask for the baby's life if she promised such a scourge of ruin on the kingdom of Ulster?

The ominous noise in the room grew louder, and one or two moved forward as if to take hold of the dangerous child and finish the deed. Then a quiet, calm voice came from the far corner.

"King Conovar MacNessa, surely in all your wisdom and experience you can find a way to keep from killing this tiny speck in the universe. At this point she is harmless. Come now, Uncle, have pity on your bard who has lost his wife and now may see his infant killed."

Conovar looked suspiciously at Fergus MacRoigh. His flattery grated on the king's ears, knowing that the red-haired man had no great admiration for him since he forced Fergus off the throne of Ulster. But the one thing that struck a note of sense was the worth of his bard. It was not wise to antagonize an ollam. Their quick-witted sarcasm and cleverly barbed verses could destroy a king quickly, diluting his power over the warriors and nobles. He must present a strong, fearless appearance before these men.

Fergus moved forward through the cluster of agitated nobles. "I can remember the way I felt when each of my three sons was placed in my hands. My heart is touched for Feilimid. See here." Boldly he took the infant out of the hand of the Druid. "See the little lass. Her soft, golden hair, and the tiny flower of a mouth. In a few years, she will be a beauty. It is a shame to kill such a one."

Conovar studied the babe. She quieted when Fergus took her gently into his two hands. She blinked a bit, revealing azure eyes.

"Indeed, I believe you are right, Fergus. Of course, I can keep her from fulfilling the curse. I fear no man, and I surely fear no squalling babe! I will send her to a crannog on a lough, far at the end of Ulster, with a nurse and a teacher. If, as you seem certain, she grows up to be a comely wench, I will wed her myself! Now, Feilimid, how say you about that plan?"

The tenderhearted bard took his tiny daughter from the large hands of Fergus MacRoigh and covered her with the hem of his cloak.

"My child would be greatly honored. My eternal thanks, King Conovar. I will miss her, but I know she will be cared for and *still live!*"

Throughout this scene, Cathbad, the Druid priest, watched in ominous silence. His dark eyes glared from under his hood as the infant was reprieved from instant death. Finally he growled, "So be it, King. Do as you will. But the day will come, you will see, when every grand thing in Ulster will come crumbling down, and you will suffer seven years without a sword in your hand or a woman in your bed!"

*   *   *

Deirdre paced the floor like a cat, a lovely cat of course. But her beauty was largely responsible for her distress. A loose gown of red silk and golden threads graced her lovely figure and enhanced the golden highlights of her hair. Every nerve in her body was alive, her arms, her hands, her trembling legs. Her brain vibrated, sending messages of restless electricity over her whole body until she thought she might burst.

"He's coming! I know he's coming soon. Oh, Lewara, I cannot bear it. That big, blonde-haired brute of a man is coming for me. I hate him! I hate the way he looks at me. I hate it when he touches me. I recoil as from a serpent. And he is going to come and claim me. Now that I have grown to a woman, he will come and take me, sure!"

"Shame, child!" Lewara, her nursemaid scolded. "Conovar MacNessa is the king. How dare you despise him. You should be proud."

"Proud, is it? To be taken off by him to some unknown place with people all around knowing what he wants with me? I would rather die!"

"Shush yourself. Don't be talking that way. Sure, you don't know how grand it will be, and the people bowing to you as his queen. Too long you have had to live out here in the wilderness with none but myself to know. It's glad I'll be to be back among people again after seventeen years alone with you in this old crannog fort. The pity is that the Druid declared you cursed when you were born. Conovar could easily have snapped your little, red neck and tossed you to the wild dogs. But your father, his favored bard, begged for your life and it was spared as long as you were exiled far away from the palace at Emania. Had King Conovar not become curious and come to see how you grew five years ago, he would never have seen your beauty. Then and there he decided that he would keep his promise and take you to himself as soon as you reached womanhood."

Deirdre's hands clenched and unclenched. "I remember the first time he saw me. And I remember every other time he came to see the way I grew. Ordering me to sit on his lap, touching me, stroking my body. Those dark blue eyes, those evil, hungry eyes. How I hate his touch." She shuddered. "Investigating how much my breasts swelled with maturity and my hips curved. I wanted to shrink back to the flat innocence of a child again."

"Now then, it's done, lass, and no use fighting him. Conovar put away his wife, Maeve. She was a beauty, too, but too bold and coarse. He will be ready to take you to fill that place at the palace, so set your mind to it and be happy."

Frustrated tears filled Deirdre's blue eyes. "Lewara, I have never seen men, only a glimpse now and then of a shepherd on the far meadow or a hunter slipping through the shadows in the woods. Are all men such as Conovar?"

"Never mind other men!" the teacher ordered. "It must be him or none, for your curse is too deadly, too evil. Only Conovar MacNessa the King can cast off the curse and change your destiny."

"The curse. How would I as an infant know of curses? And how would I become a curse to him? If he would leave me alone, never would I go near him to do him harm. But if he takes me, I will hate him forever and do all that I can to torment him."

With those words, Deirdre marched out of the big,

round, wooden hut and crossed the courtyard of the island. Through the gates of the stockade she strode, her
long, slim legs taking her swiftly across the narrow
causeway to the lake shore. Once on the bank, she
gazed around, deciding where she must go to find some
kind of comfort.

The trees in the forest reminded her of the dark
captivity she was destined to suffer. She chose the
meadow, climbing the hill under a wide, open sky. In
the distance, the blue-purple mountains rose in breathtaking, giant mounds. Beyond those gentle peaks lay an
unspeakably endless expanse of green water, Lewara
said. If only she could reach that water and sail away on
it, away from the disgusting lechery of the king.

Around her skirts, wild flowers and heather grew in
tall grass. The scent of the blossoms and the fresh grass
filled her with hope. She raised her young arms to the
wide heavens, reaching for the blessings of the goddess
Danu to save her from her fated future.

As she reached the top of the lea, she was startled to
see a figure, a young man, lying against his elbow on
the ground. He held a harp in his hands and began to
strum it softly. Surprise almost sent Deirdre running
away in fear, but curiosity and loneliness made her
stand still and watch him.

He did not see her immediately, concentrating on
his music. As she watched him, she felt a warm affection
for the young fellow. His dark hair was drawn back in a
tightly bound clump. He was clean shaven, as all the
warriors were, the better to keep a foe from yanking his
beard and slashing off his head. She was sure he was a
warrior in the service of the king. He wore studded

leather armor. At his waist hung a sling and a bag of iron balls. Beside him on the grass lay a short, razor-sharp sword.

Deirdre watched his fine, clean muscles move in time to the music he played. How good it would be if such a man would protect her from the ugly, boorish Conovar.

Of course, a warrior was not able to provide her with grand gowns of silk and linen, intricate golden chains and brooches, such as Conovar often brought to her, grooming her for the palace. But what need had she for such things if she got away from the brute?

She sighed. The young man looked up. Alarm appeared on his face. He knew who she was. Everyone knew about the beautiful maiden who had been in exile since birth on the testimony of a Druid priest. No one dared search her out or speak to her. She belonged to King Conovar, his liege.

Quickly he turned away his head. "Banshee," he whispered.

So he would not speak to her. No one would. Deirdre sighed once more and snapped a wild rose off a nearby briar. Walking slowly forward she dropped the flower at his feet and moved on in resigned silence.

He stood up. "Come back, lovely lady," he said. "What harm can there be in a few words?"

Deirdre stopped and turned toward him. "You called me Banshee," she said. "Why did you call me that?"

"Because the faery woman cries when someone is about to die and, sure, I could die for speaking to you."

"Then go." She turned to walk away. His words sounded grand and his clean, young body was so fine.

Her heart was breaking for never having heard such a voice before. He spoke the truth; he could lose his head just for speaking to her, a girl who had been in bonded seclusion all her life, pledged to the king by fate. She would not put the life of such a fine, young man in danger.

"Wait, beautiful lady. I will talk to you. Naisi MacUisnach fears nothing, not even the displeasure of Conovar MacNessa."

So, they sat themselves down on a gray stone outcropping where they could see far across the meadows and the powerful beauty of the dark green mountain and a silver lake below. They talked together.

Words spilled out of Deirdre, bitter words saved up from all the lonely days of her life. Naisi asked questions, a quiet, gentle inquisition. He was appalled at the terrible loneliness of the lass hidden away for seventeen years with none but an old woman to listen to her sorrow.

"This must not continue," he said. "The Red Knights are a noble, gallant corps. They will surely defend you."

"The Red Knights are sworn allegiance to the king of Ulster, as you yourself must surely be. They will not oppose him for the sake of one woman, and one who is cursed at that. No, it will not continue. Conovar will take me to his mansion at Emania. There I will be used by him and paraded before people in my shame. Now that he has divorced Queen Maeve, there is nothing to stop him. I will not do it." She rose up. "I will drown myself and die!"

Before he could stop her, Deirdre took off running down the slope toward the watery depths of the lake. It took only seconds for Naisi to catch her and wrap his strong arms around her, keeping her from suicide. She wept on his breast.

"Deirdre, beautiful, innocent Deirdre, I will not let this come to pass. My two brothers and I will be your champions, your defenders. We will protect you."

"You cannot. No one dares to help me. He will kill you all. I won't let you die for me!"

"You will come with me *now!*"

He led her away.

When his two brothers, Ainley and Ardan, saw him coming to the fortified rath where they lived with their father, with Deirdre on his arm, they were alarmed. They, too, were proud warriors, pledged to serve Conovar MacNessa and the kingdom of Ulster. The fortress of Uisnach had always held men of honor. Naisi was bringing disgrace upon them.

"Are you mad?" Ardan declared. "Don't you know this is the lass betrothed to King Conovar? Get her back to where you found her or we will be executed, and rightly so!"

Ainley was equally stunned at his older brother's foolishness and said so in no uncertain words.

"Wait, brothers," Naisi begged. "Hear her story and then decide whether or not you will give her protection from Conovar. But first, we must take her some place where she can hide. Too many eyes and ears here in the fort."

They slipped her away from the rath to a cave on the side of a mountain, a shelter created by a huge, stone shelf, a place where they could see any intruders coming from far away. Deirdre told them about all of her fear and distress and a lifetime of smothered discipline.

"I bore it well," she said, her eyes lowered to her fingers smoothing the folds of the rich, silk gown. "I knew no other life, and I was content. But then he began coming to watch me. Conovar, the evil, old lecher, big, heavy hands fondling my body, lips slavering with disgusting lust. I hate him. I cannot bear it, and I will kill myself before I will let him take me to Emania with him!"

"He had a good wife," Ardan commented. "Maeve was grand, a woman of power. The Red Branch had great respect for her and would have followed her into battle any time."

"And that is the reason he discarded her," Naisi said. "He feared her power to control his own forces. He divorced her, but I feel that it would have been she who did the act soon. She was a princess and had her own heritage waiting for her in Connaught."

"Well now," Ainley said with resolution. "For Deirdre's sake and for the sake of our brother who is clearly captivated by the lovely maiden, we must go along and help her to get far from Emania and the king of Ulster."

Ardan rubbed his chin and frowned. "You know what this means. We will be counted as traitors, foolish men who, for the sake of a woman, will have denied our vows to the king and left the honor of our father, Uisnach, and family and become fugitives."

"Then you will not do it? You will not go with Deirdre and stand as her protector?" Naisi asked.

"And who said that?" Ainley objected. "Of course we will go to protect the lady fair."

Ardan sighed deeply. "Indeed we will go, for our brother and for the lady."

The sons of Uisnach gathered together their weapons and provisions and left Ulster. They cut their way through deep, green forests and over bogs and streams, selling their services to one grateful king after another. And always, Conovar's warriors came down on the province in which they dwelled and threatened to destroy the kingdom that gave Deirdre sanctuary.

Her life was not easy. They lived in caves or crude, stone beehive huts. Deirdre was unused to drawing water and cooking and sleeping on soiled sheepskins full of fleas. But she complained not at all. Weren't the three wonderful warriors giving up their honor as champions of Ulster in order to help her? Were they not also having to live under miserable conditions when their father's fort was rich and filled with food and comfort? And were they not suffering all of this dishonor and discomfort for her sake?

At last, Naisi told his brothers, "We have run out of land. No king will hire us now, threatened with being attacked by the Red Branch Knights for the sake of a woman. Our only refuge may be to go by boat across the Giant's Causeway to Alba and beg service to the king there."

The brothers outfitted Deirdre in a simple, woolen robe that hid her graceful figure and a hood for her head that hung darkly over her face. The four traveled over great, stony, green mountains to the northern coast and found ship. Within three days, they set foot on the rocky, wild shore of Alba. They ate deer and hare roasted over campfires as they traveled across the wind-beaten, dark moors to the castle of the Scottish king. The three brothers presented themselves to the king of the Scots, and he was pleased to take on such fine warriors.

A simple, round hut was built by the brothers a bit farther away from the rest of the village. There they settled, Deirdre and her husband, Naisi, and the brothers Ardan and Ainley. Often they were called out to fight the ferocious, painted Picts. Naisi forbid Deirdre to step outside the hut during the day, especially while the brothers were gone to battle.

"Once you are seen, your beauty will be coveted," he told her tenderly. "I cannot promise that these wild Scots will not kill us and take you to be used worse than Conovar MacNessa's purposes."

For a year, the family lived in Alba. Then, one early morning, the Scottish king's steward was walking among the village homes and happened on the hut that stood out away from the rest. Curious, he peeked inside to see who lived there. His eyes opened wide.

On one side of the hut, on beds of sheepskin, the two brothers slept. He knew them well. A pair of fine mercenaries serving his king. On the opposite side lay the champion, Naisi, and by his side the most lovely woman the steward had ever seen. Silken, blonde hair spread across the woolen bolster, long lashes lay on soft, white cheeks just touched with a blush of rose. Her heavy robe had been discarded for comfort while she slept, and the intruding man beheld an exquisite figure in soft, white linen, white ankles and delicate feet revealed.

Quickly he left and rushed to the king. "You have

been searching for a woman fit to be your queen. I have found the most perfect creature I have ever seen. She belongs to the warrior, Naisi."

"Is she so beautiful indeed? Then I must have her," the giant, red-haired king grinned. "But I will not challenge Naisi for her. I want her to come to me willingly. I will not have a stubborn, unhappy bride. Go to her while Naisi is away and persuade her to come to me. Surely she will not deny the king's request and the opportunity to become queen."

"Of course she will come. I'm sure of it!"

The steward watched carefully and approached Deirdre while the brothers were gone. Deirdre tried to hide in the shadows of the hut, but the steward called out, "Beautiful lady, come and speak to me. The king wants to meet you, for I have told him of your great loveliness. Would you like to be the bride of the king?"

"I have a husband," she said softly. "I cannot be the bride of the king."

"The King can make short work of Naisi. Come with me to the king."

"No," she said. "No."

He went back again. Then again. Then again. He told her of the wealth and comforts of the castle, of the adoration the king would lavish upon her.

She said, "No."

The Scottish king became impatient. "If she is all you promised, then I want her. If you cannot bring her willingly, then we will have to be certain that Naisi and his brothers die in battle. See to it!"

Deirdre could see a change in the steward's demeanor when he came once more. He was not so polite or imploring. His manner was brisk. She detected a final demand in his words, a sense of "come to the king or else."

That night she told the brothers. The next morning the steward found the hut empty. Without another alternative, they took to the island of Tory. The stony caves were their shelter. But they never spoke of their hardships nor blamed Deirdre. She wept sometimes in shame for causing them so much distress. Surely, she had to relieve them of their wonderful loyalty and kindness. She must die.

One day, Ardan walked among the rocky cliffs above the shore of Tory Island hunting diligently for birds eggs. His stomach ached with yearning for a hearty, roasted shank of venison or bacon off the side of a wild boar. Neither were to be found on the cold, bare, windy isle. So, to snare an occasional puffin or gull was their only opportunity to have meat. The rest of the time, they resorted to raiding eggs from nests tucked into the sheer sides of the rocks. The sharp winds of the sea penetrated his leather armor and the heavy, wool tunic beneath it and burned his gaunt cheeks to bright red.

A bit of white caught his wind-stung eyes as he looked ahead, searching the land for nesting places. Ardan reached for the scrap of white linen blowing in the grasses, shredded by gorse. He took it up in his stiff, cold hands, bloodied by birds' angry pecks, and almost lost it as it tried to fly away in the wind.

Holding the cloth closer, he recognized it as that with which Deirdre had hooded her head while gathering wads of grass for fire that morning. He remembered her eyes were puffy and stained from tears that she shed nightly. Naisi tried to console her, but she continually chastised herself for bringing such hardship on the three fine champions.

What would Deirdre be doing out here in the miserable wind so close to the sea? The brothers did the foraging, admonishing her to keep inside and safe, if not warm and comfortable. Their lives were devoted to her. Their success in keeping her from being ravaged by lust-crazed kings was all that kept them going.

Ardan made his way over the next stony rise. Then he stopped. Deirdre was on her knees at the very edge of an earthy precipice, her arms raised in an attitude of supplication. Her voice came barely audible through the sounds of ocean and gale as she murmured chanting words. The she rose to her feet and he saw her lean forward, toward the open air above the beckoning ocean roar.

He rushed to her, grasping her shoulders against faltering over the edge. Using all his strength he tugged her backward, away from the crumbling rim that could give way and send them both plummeting to their death on the rocks below.

"Deirdre!" he shouted, pulling her back from the cliff. "Deirdre, *ban dahr!* My sister, what are you doing?"

"Let me go!" Her hair whipped across her face and her blue eyes were wide with determination. "You must let me do it. I have promised Danu that I will give myself to her in the depths of the ocean if she will take Naisi and you and Ainley back to Eire in peace. I am the only thing in the way!"

"No! I won't let you. Don't you see that you are the reason we have life? As long as we can protect you, it gives us a mission, a noble cause. We are warriors, trained to bear hardship and tribulation. Without you, we would flounder."

"You don't understand, Ardan. It will never come to good! I have seen a vision of the blood of my husband and his kinsmen on the grounds of Emania, on the hem of my skirt, on the palms of my hands! I have seen the eyes of lecherous Conovar laughing down on you and me, hysterical with joy at blood and death and horror!" She began to weaken and cry, trembling limbs wanting to sink onto the turf once more. "I cannot go on; I will not let you sacrifice your lives any longer for me. I will trade my life to the goddess Danu for you."

"No, Deirdre, you will not do this!"

"I must! I cannot bear to watch my beloved Naisi and you and Ainley suffer hunger and harsh weather out here on this rocky island. Without me, you can go back to Eire, live with your father, serve any king you want. There is no end to this life out here, no relief. I must be gone!"

Suddenly the wind carried sounds over the scrubby island. Ardan and Deirdre turned to see three figures coming toward them, voices raised in excitement.

"Ardan! See here!" called Ainley. "Naisi found Fergus MacRoigh beaching his curragh on the far side of Tory. Good news!"

"Good news? Has Conovar died?" Deirdre's heart leaped with hope.

The trio came closer. Naisi laughed. "Not quite that good. But things have changed."

Fergus smiled. He gazed at the lovely, young woman and remembered the terrified, squalling infant he held nineteen years ago. Now she was ragged and hungry, a fugitive from home, a child of sorrow. His voice became low and tender.

"The nobles at Conovar's court have shamed him. They know how you have suffered, how all four of you have struggled to keep you, Deirdre, from having to live with a stubborn, vindictive old fool. They have made him promise you all safe passage home to Emania, and a return to normal life in service to your king, for you grand young warriors. And, lass, he agrees that he will honor your marriage to Naisi."

The brothers shouted for joy. Going home to Eire. To pride and loyalty and comforts. And no more fear for Deirdre. But Deirdre stood still, watching them, and the tears started again.

Naisi became annoyed. "Why do you weep more?" he demanded. "All is well at last. Come and be happy with us!"

"I don't trust him. I know him well. And I have seen visions, horrible visions. No, we must not go back. Never!"

Fergus MacRoigh stroked his beard, the flame-colored hair now streaked with gray. He studied the girl, his green eyes soft with understanding.

"I cannot blame you, lass. We have both had experience with his treachery. This I will do. I will pledge my own honor that you will go to Emania and be safe. I have three fine sons, Fiacha, Borb, and Illan. I am very proud of my sons and love them just as your father, Feilimid, loved you. I give you my sons' pledges also."

For just a minute, Deirdre looked into the eyes of the kind noble and felt relief. Then the sickening visions came back and she wailed, "No! No, no. I see a scarlet cloud over Emania, dripping blood onto the lawns of the palace. I will not go back. The sons of Uisnach must not go back!"

Pressured by hunger and cold, the brothers scoffed at her warnings.

Taking her in his strong arms, Naisi said, "He would not dare hurt us or you, my lovely Deirdre. His nobles would not let him. They are good men. If they offer us refuge in our home country, we will go, and gladly."

All Deirdre's weeping pleas would not change their minds. They rejoiced. They were determined to go home.

"You should have seen them, the nobles, pleading your need," Fergus told them over a smoky fire in the cave that evening. "The three finest warriors of Erin, they told him, would secure your victory against all the threats of other kings. Here they are, the sons of Uisnach, living on a bare island, of no use to anyone, all because you desire Deirdre. Bring them back to Emania. Forgive them royally. Everyone will admire you for your generosity, and you will have the best of all armies of Erin, they said. He finally agreed."

"It's going to be grand," a delighted Naisi told his brothers as he broke open a fire-blackened roasted egg. "We will once more give allegiance to our own king and Ulster. We will see our father and be no more a shame to him. All will be good, my beautiful Deirdre."

"Not so," she persisted. "I know that evil Conovar. He cannot be trusted. I could not bear it if something happened to you. And your brothers have stood strong beside us through all of these hardships. They will be in danger. Please, let us not go to Emania!"

Naisi was too happy to allow Deirdre's womanly worries to sway his decision. "Don't be fretting now, my pretty bride. Fergus MacRoigh is an honest man, a man to be trusted with your life. He promises that Conovar will forgive. Let us go back to our homeland and family."

Fergus left the young people to gather their pitiable possessions while he went to Emania and reported the success of his mission to the king. Conovar was pleased.

"We must prepare a feast of welcome for them," he told Fergus. "I want you to be here waiting for them when they arrive at the mansion."

"I want to go out and meet them, Conovar. I am happy to be the one to bring them home, and I want to see them first."

"Don't worry about that. Send an emissary to bring them up. Tell your emissary to meet them at the second walled rampart outside the city and lead them to the mansion for the feast. We will welcome them here."

Reluctantly, Fergus obeyed. He wanted badly to see to Naisi and Ardan and Ainley and Deirdre as soon as they made their way home, but Conovar would have his way. So be it. It was after all a small matter. He would send his sons, Fiacha, Borb, and Illan, to take his place and greet them.

As soon as Fergus left the room, Conovar called Eogan MacDuracht to his side. Eogan was tall and wiry, his thin straggling beard was dirty brown, and he had small eyes that were a mix of brown and green. He was the son of Conovar's enemy king, Duracht of Farney, and had long been a deadly enemy of Conovar's. Many a bloody battle they fought against each other. However, they seemed to find a curious kinship in each other's deceitful and ruthless schemes, and lately had decided to become friends.

Slyly, Conovar said, "Would you like to prove your friendship to me? When the sons of Uisnach get to the second rampart from the palace, take your men and kill them there. Do not let any of the slightest harm come to Deirdre, not one scratch. I want her as beautiful as the last day I saw her. But I want Naisi and his brothers slaughtered like pigs!"

An evil smile crossed Eogan's face. "It's a pleasant task you give me, one in which I will take grand delight."

On the journey across the northern part of Erin to the city of Emania, Deirdre could not rest. Three times she woke screaming in the night. In her dreams, she saw the cloud of blood over Emania. But Naisi calmed her, gently scolding that her mania of fear of Conovar was making her frenetic. She must be happy that they were going home after two miserable years of flight.

Fiacha and his brothers were delighted to have the honor of greeting the king's guests. By the time the sons of Uisnach and Dierdre arrived at the second green rampart that circled the royal hill of Emania Macha, the MacRoighs were waiting for them with a handful of young friends. They welcomed them heartily, laughing, slapping backs playfully, a jolly group.

Deirdre sat on the wall, silent, her thin hands clasped tightly in her lap, her terrified eyes staring ahead, seeing yet the cloud of blood over the palace. Her face was dead white, her blue eyes wide with dread.

Suddenly, over the first rampart, riders came racing

across the field. Eogan and his company rode down on the little group, heading for the brothers. Quickly all the young men, totally unprepared for battle, began to fight, struggling to relieve Eogan's men of their swords, but it was impossible.

Fiacha, seeing their purpose, leaped over and knocked down Naisi, covering his body with his own. With glee, Eogan rammed his spear through the boy's back and into Naisi's body, killing them both.

By the time Eogan's warriors were finished, the ground was covered with bloody bodies of young men, sliced and slaughtered, a sight of horror. Only Deirdre stood, her face gray, paralyzed, her body cold as death. Eogan reached down and yanked her up onto his horse and carried her to the palace.

In the great hall of the palace, Conovar MacNessa hosted a feast, a "welcome" for the sons of Uisnach and Deirdre. As many as fifty revelers ate and drank heartily. A few knew the supposed purpose of the festivities. Most knew not nor cared as long as the wine and mead flowed. Conovar himself seemed full of gladness, toasting and eating, a wonder to his subjects who knew his demanding, hateful temperament.

In his seat at the banquet table, Fergus MacRoigh looked puzzled. He watched Conovar carefully, trying to figure why the king was in such grand spirits. Logically, the man would have kept control of his behavior at this time. It was an occasion for studied diplomacy, three warriors returning to their king's service after years of traitorous rebellion. King Conovar should have been weighing the words he was going to say.

And Deirdre. How would the king behave toward

the maiden who had despised his offer to be consort to the king of Ulster? How might he maintain his dignity and respect? Instead of considering these things, Conovar was enjoying himself with great abandon.

A young slave in a coarse, woolen tunic slipped into the hall and scurried around the wall until he was behind the king. Leaning over his shoulder, the boy whispered something. Conovar stood up, delight in his liquor-glassy, blue eyes.

He raised his pitcher of mead. "Honor!" he shouted. "Honor to the great King Conovar MacNessa, the most powerful king in Eire. The king who never fails to reward those who do not give him homage. Honor!"

What did he mean? Fergus felt his face go numb. Where were Deirdre and the brothers? Where were *his* sons? He rose from his chair, ready to rush out to the ramparts. Then he dropped back into his seat.

The wide, oaken doors of the great hall were flung open. A cluster of warriors, sweating from exertion and exhilarated by battle, spattered with fresh, red blood, burst into the room. Before them they propelled their battle prize, Deirdre!

Behind them, proud and amused, strode Eogan MacDuracht on his long, bare legs, his ragged cloak hanging limp from splashes of blood.

The fighting men let go of their captive, rushing to grab pitchers of mead to quench the thirst from their labors. Deirdre would have sunk to the floor had not Eogan reached out and held her up.

"Your trophy, Conovar! Here she is in good condition as ordered!"

"At last. Deirdre, my lass, you will be grateful to me

for setting you free from poverty and toil. We will have grand times, you and me." He licked his wet lips.

Deirdre pulled herself up tall. Her gown was covered with blood, the blood of her husband, her Naisi. Her hands were red from holding his body while around her the screams of the young people being murdered shot lightning through her head.

Slowly she held out her palms toward Conovar. Her blue eyes never left his face as she gathered wetness from the folds of her gown. Then she pulled aside the neck of her gown, revealing white skin, and with her forefinger, she made a scarlet cross on her flesh.

The room was in turmoil. Some revelers wanted to know what had happened. Others already knew and merrily drank the toast to the king. In the confusion, Fergus MacRoigh got himself up from his seat again and made his way through the crowd and out the doors.

He found the body of his son, Fiacha, the boy's valor proven by the position in which he lay, impaled trying to save the life of the one he and his father had sworn to protect. His two other sons' bodies lay sprawled among those on the bloody grass of the rampart.

Unspeakable agony filled the father. Soon it was joined by fiery hot fury. Conovar MacNessa, the king so admired by many, had deliberately sent Fergus's sons to their death. Conovar had used Fergus's reputation as an honest man to lure Deirdre and the sons of Uisnach into his trap. Knowing full well what was going to happen, the king had sent Eogan and his men to murder Naisi and his brothers and everyone else who was found on the second rampart, including Fergus's own children!

Within days, Fergus had pulled together his own loyal army of three thousand warriors and rode in attack on Emania Macha. He was beaten back, but not before the palace was almost destroyed by fire and the liar Conovar had fled for his life. The king would come back later to restore Emania to its glory.

Exhausted and heartsick, Fergus gathered his family and troops and left for Connaught. Maeve, the rambunctious queen, would greet him gladly as an additional ally and would happily welcome his small army to join her own. Someday Fergus knew Maeve would repay Conovar for putting her away by divorce. He vowed in his heart to be a part of her vengeance by every strength he had.

For a full year, Deirdre lived under Conovar's power. The maids gowned her in finery, hung jewels on her, and dressed her silky, golden hair in elaborate styles. She spoke not one word. He arranged magnificent entertainment for her, music and bards and fools. Her downcast eyes saw none of them, only the bloody body of her beloved Naisi lying on the ramparts of Emania. Sometimes she wept helpless, frustrated sobs, which earned her only ranting shouts and threats from the king. She was there, in his bed, limp and at his mercy every night. She was used brutally, but without satisfaction by Conovar.

At last he wearied of her. Her red eyes and tears, her silence, her apathy. He called Eogan to him.

"I have come to hate Deirdre. She lies in bed with her hands folded, looking at the roof, wilted. I had grand hopes while I watched her grow up and bloom and become more beautiful and voluptuous. I dreamed

of having that glorious creature to myself. I rid myself of that troublesome Maeve in preparation for Deirdre to come to my bed. Now I have nothing but a thin, limp wench that never speaks or moves. I hate her!"

A wicked leer spread across Eogan's face. "Conovar, let me have her. I will take her for a year. I will train her. In one year, I will bring her back to you fair game for a romp, that I promise!" Eogan's eyes grew steel hard. "If I do not make a change in her, if she remains sullen and morose, she will be sorry that she despised the pleasures of Eogan. She may come back to you without breath in her body."

"Go along with her then. I have my eye on Maeve's sister, Ethne. She is a mousy thing compared to Maeve, but she is agreeable and I am tired of stubborn women."

Deirdre was placed in the back of a chariot with a bag full of grand gowns and gifts. Eogan, in the front, whipped the horses. Conovar stood beside him, casting insults over his shoulder at the helpless, young woman.

"Wait until you taste of Eogan's skills in breaking horses," he shouted. "We will share your charms once you are properly trained. You are a ewe between two healthy rams!"

Conovar continued to harass and torment Deirdre as the chariot bumped over hill and stream on its way to Eogan's fort.

Then she spoke, the first words Conovar had heard from her in a year. Her voice was hoarse and hard. The determination in it sounded like stone.

"The curse, Conovar MacNessa. The curse that caused you to put me away for seventeen years, never to know father nor mother nor kin. Do you remember the curse?"

"So now you speak! The curse? Oh, indeed, I recall it." Conovar sneered. "Cathbad said you would be the cause of the death of the three finest warriors in Ulster. You were."

Horrible pain shot through Deirdre's heart. He told it true. She had been the cause of the death of Naisi and Ainley and Ardan, the three champions of Ulster, just as the Druid had predicted. She wished she were dead. But not until she sent fear into Conovar, dread of the future.

"You forget the rest." Deirdre's voice was tight with hate. There was an eerie note that should have warned him that something was to come. "The Druid said that Emania Macha would burn."

"So it did. And so I have built it back, grander than ever!"

"But not before much that was treasure was destroyed. Do you remember the best of the curse, O King? For seven years, you will live but without a sword in your hand or a woman in your bed. *Seven years!*"

Enraged, Conovar turned himself around, his face contorted with fury, reaching out his big hand to strike her.

Then quickly, Deirdre stood up, tall, regal, in the chariot. Her rich, purple cloak swirled around her in the wind. They were coming near to a pile of stones with one huge, sharp, white stone on top, an ancient sacrificial altar to the goddess Danu.

Deirdre of the Sorrows raised her arm, a long, white finger pointing to the startled king.

"Conovar MacNessa, the curse I was born to bring upon you, the curse that has proven true by your own evil hands, that curse I set upon you forever. *Remember it!*"

With that, she leaped headlong from the carriage, aiming for the waiting white altar. She struck it squarely, crushing her head, a burst of scarlet blood splashing over her silken, golden hair.

❦

Conovar married Ethne. It was not until many years later that Queen Maeve of Connaught went to war with Ulster to improve her herds of cattle. Conovar was injured in a battle at the River Breffney. Maeve's champion, Keat, skilled with the sling, shot a ball of iron deep into the king's brain. His physician, Faith Liag, was unable to remove the ball without causing instant death to Conovar. So the king was obliged to curb all physical and passionate activity in order to remain among the living. He could not arrogantly lead his army into battles, he could not become emotionally distressed, he could not take part in physical relations with his wife. He sank deeper and deeper into dreary dolefulness. Life was not worth living.

Then a day came when the sky went black and the earth shook, lightning crashed and thunder roared in the sky. He begged old Cathbad to explain the horrifying events. The seer told him that in the Far East, a good man had been tortured by Roman soldiers and killed upon a strange instrument of ex-

ecution, a cross. The gods were ready to destroy the world for the evil deed.

Conovar leaped to his feet and grabbed his sword where it hung for seven years on the wall of the palace of Emania. "Take me to them! I will kill the Romans! I am Conovar MacNessa the King!" He raised the sword high over his head, brandishing it wildly, shaking his body in fury.

Then a small iron ball fell to the floor and rolled away. Conovar saw it, stunned, before he fell to the floor, dead.

The voice of Cathbad quoting the curse of Dierdre seemed to echo through the great hall of Emania.

Bridget, the Saint

No anthology of Irish women would be complete without relating the life of the most beloved, productive, and determined female child of God that ever was in Ireland. Bridget had been influenced by the words of St. Patrick. She had one goal in life: to relieve the suffering of the poor and ill. She did it, too, with total disregard for the right to own riches and authority of the pompous wealthy. She was delightfully brazen! Being born on the wrong side of the blanket, she experienced both poverty and pampering, and decided to follow in the footsteps of the Master.

"mam, why must you work so hard while the mistress does nothing all day?"

Brocessa raised up from scrubbing the stone floor of the great hall of Tir-Conaill. She arched her back and rubbed it, looking lovingly at her three-year-old daughter sitting beside her.

"My little Bridget, someday you will understand that

there are but two kinds of people in the world. Now, there are ones like me who were born into bondage and will never get out. And there are ones who are afflicted with crippled bones or ailing bodies and cannot work to earn a living. Many there are who have no dwelling to keep them from the rains and cold and no patch of earth to grow food. All of us are the poor. Then there are the high ones, those who own lands and take tribute from the poor and rule the country. They are the rich."

"But Patrick, the man of God who came to us walking out of the forest, said that Jesus felt sorry for the poor. He healed them. He gave them food. Should not the rich then do good things for the poor?"

Brocessa smiled at the innocent truth spoken by the tiny maid. She dried her hands on her coarse, woolen skirt and put an arm around her little girl.

"Truth you said, sure. We were blessed that Patrick came our way on his journeys across Eire. Remember that truth when you grow up and go back to your father's house. He is rich. Claim your heritage, but never forget to follow the example of Christ."

A harsh voice burst into the gentle advice of Bridget's mother. "Brocessa, stop filling the child's head with foolish hopes," shouted Tay, the wife of the Druid priest of Tir-Conaill. "You know she is bound to my husband as much as you yourself are bound. It seems you have too much time on your hands if you can stop your work to preach. And, if Bridget can understand you at three years old, then she can understand orders. She should be working, too. Listen to me," she came across the room and took the child by her thin, little arm.

"Get yourself out to the field and tell the work master to make you useful. Get now! And you, Brocessa, get back to your own work!"

Bridget ran on her short legs out a door at the side of the great room, and Brocessa leaned back over her mopping rag and pail, tears stinging her eyes for her tiny child. Up to now, Tay had allowed Bridget to stay at her mother's side while she worked. Now the little girl would be slaving like Brocessa herself.

But she was glad of the things she had said. Indeed, Bridget's father was Duvah, a prince in the line of kings of Leinster. An affection had grown in Brocessa for her big, handsome lord. While she lived in his servitude, he sometimes came to her in the night. She welcomed him. Indeed it would have done no good to resist, for he was her owner, she was his slave, and he had the right. But he took her gently. And she quietly accepted the fact that, no matter what passed between them, she must never show any sign of affection or familiarity during the daylight hours when her slim, young body was bent under hard work.

When the little maid found herself pregnant, somehow a singular delight and contentment came upon her and could be seen in her soft, blue eyes and innocent smiles. Brocessa held the precious burden inside her secretly, until it became too obvious to hide.

Duvah's childless wife found out. It was not too hard to know that on those long nights when her own bed was empty, her husband had been lying beside a petty slave in a hovel. She was livid. "Get her out of here!" she demanded. "The harlot. I can't bear the sight of her!"

He did that. He sold the lass, Brocessa, with child,

like a mare in foal, to a wealthy Druid living at Tir-Conaill near Dundalk in County Louth. And there the baby, Bridget, was born.

Strangely, Illan, the Druid, made a prophecy to Bridget's father when he bought her. "Duvah, I see a strange thing in the fog of time. The seed of your wife shall serve the seed of the bondmaid, for she will bring forth a daughter—remarkable, radiant, who will shine greatest among all the stars."

Duvah went home puzzling over the prophecy, but prepared to forget about the sweet, dark-haired bond-maid and do proper service to the wife his father had arranged for him. It was his duty to raise up sons to carry on the family heritage.

The girl had never forgotten her mother's words, repeated often as they lay side by side on a bed of rushes in the wattled slaves hut. When Bridget was nine years old, cleaning the mistress's chamber, she came upon a fine brooch set with expensive stones. Her blue eyes widened. "Why, just one of these stones would feed a poor family for a year!"

Later that day, she was bidden to go to the clachan that sat on the banks of the lough and demand tribute to the House of Tir-Conaill from the fishermen there. On her arm she carried a huge basket. Passing through the village of wattle-and-daub shacks and stone beehive huts, she saw children sitting in the dirt, their bodies thin with hunger. Old, toothless widows begged for bread from the mothers in the clachan who did not have enough to feed their own children. Grudgingly, the fishermen gave Bridget a basket of the hard-won catch it had taken them an entire day to gather, fish that could have fed their children that night.

Her heart became heavy to see their misery. So many hungry people. And so many grand, sparkling stones in that golden brooch of her mistress.

With the basket on her arm, Bridget marched to the big house with its large, wood-paneled rooms, soft pillows, and full pantries. As soon as she left the fish in the keeping room, she went to the chamber of the mistress. Digging through the casket of brilliant jewelry, she found it. She proceeded to pry out the stones, one by one.

She left the golden pin full of tiny hollows and went back to the village. Searching out the poorest, the most ragged and hungry, she left a gleaming gem in each hand. The stunned people thanked her profusely.

"Don't be thanking me," she said kindly. "Give thanks to the Lord God and His Son for making them available. Now, get you to the gombeenman and sell them to buy food."

When Illan and Tay found the skeletal remains of the expensive pin, Bridget did not deny her culpability. They were aghast! How dare the slave maid steal from them so boldly. And for what purpose? To feed the poor. It was useless effort. There were too many poor to make any difference.

"You stupid, thieving child!" Tay screamed. "You will be beaten for this! I will have your face branded a thief! You shall have the fingers of your left hand cut off!"

The Druid stared at the girl silently, shocked at her audacity. Then he spoke, "I remember a vision I had when Duvah first brought me her mother, who was with child. I had forgotten until now. Yes, wife, she must be punished. We will have her whipped with three thongs only. We dare not have her maimed or branded. Go now, Bridget. Suffer the pain of punishment and stop your evil, thieving ways."

So Bridget, nine years old, was thoroughly whipped. Then she was cut loose from the flogging post, tears streaming down her cheeks, and raised her hands to the sky, praising Christ for allowing her to suffer pain for obedience to Him.

Bridget continued to grow up as a bondservant to the Druid and Tay. First she carried sheaves of grain in her tiny arms. Then she was put to work tending sheep. Finally, she was old enough to become the dairy maid, milking cows, skimming the milk to make butter and curds.

As she grew older, Bridget became more beautiful. Her soft, brown hair had a halo of golden sheen. Her skin was smooth and delicately tan from spending time in the wonderful outdoors. Her cheeks had the soft glow of rose. It was her blue eyes that gave her an almost ethereal radiance. The farm work exhilarated her young body.

She loved it. Out in the open air of the countryside of Eire, Bridget toiled happily. Jesus, the Master, had talked of "fields white to the harvest." He spoke of His followers as "sheep," and Bridget delighted in the frolics of the foolish, thoughtless lambs. The cows, the big boes, were huge and plodding, welcoming her strong, young hands as she relieved their swollen udders.

There was something so satisfying, so gloriously primeval, in bringing forth food from the meadows and fields. Even the thick, green forest that covered the island of Eire yielded acorns and healing herbs. The Great God had made the earth to give sustenance to all creatures, and Bridget gladly did the toil that caused it to come forth.

The Land. The beautiful green land of Eire. The wild, high sky often heavy with powerful, blue-black clouds and rainbows and, at night, overwhelmed her with millions of stars. Bridget's heart was made for Eire.

Brocessa was still young, but the hard work had made her dark hair go gray. Cold water for scrubbing made her hands swell with arthritis, and her poor, raw knees were swollen and red from the stone floors.

Her mother's situation saddened Bridget. The girl had helped many people in every way she could, but she could not help her mother become free of bondage and overwork. She prayed that someday she might be able to make life better for the tender, little woman.

She was fourteen when the Druid noticed that the butter from her creamery was dwindling. Secretly, Bridget would take the day's yield of rich, pale butter and divide it into twelve balls, one for each of the disciples for the house and a big one representing Jesus. That big one she gave to the poor. According to her reading of the Holy Writ, "Christ is in the person of the least of these."

One day, Illan and Tay decided to go down to the dairy to see for themselves why the produce was not equal to the number of cows. They walked down the slope from the tall, oaken mansion, past chickens scratching in the black mud and dogs sleeping against the haggard hayrick. When they came to the little log cabin built half under the ground where the milk cooled and the butter was kneaded and rolled, they called to Bridget.

"I know exactly how much butter should be coming out of here!" the Druid declared.

"I want butter balls for the house and I want this basket filled now!" demanded his wife.

Bridget smiled and went inside the little dairy house. She knew that there were only one and a half balls of butter left there. How would she fill the basket on her mistress's arms with only one and a half balls of the rich, oily stuff? As she moved she prayed, *hard*, asking the Prince of Heaven to provide.

She took the ball and a half to her mistress and placed them in the basket. Then she went back inside and there, lying on the smooth, wooden table, another ball and a half lay! She carried them out to add to the two pieces already there.

"Why do you bring only one and a half each time?" Tay demanded.

"I have only two hands," Bridget responded. "Be patient, Mistress Tay, and I will fill your basket with God's bounty."

Time after time she entered the cooling room and found one and a half balls of butter waiting on the heavy, wooden table. The basket was filled.

The Druid murmured, "If every basket in the county were given to her, she would fill them all. It is a miracle!"

His wife took the basket to the house, but the Druid stood there yet, staring at the happy, little dairy maid. At last he said, "I fear to have you near me. My god Bel and the powers of darkness cannot bear your light. You should be serving Patrick's God, whom I dread. Take my cows and all of their butter."

Bridget stopped her work and gazed at the master. "Keep your cows," she said, "and give me my mother's freedom!"

Bridget was set free, too. She settled her mother with the nuns in the Abbey of St. Francis, to rest and regain her health. Then it was time for her to go to her father's house, as her mother had told her many times she must do. She went, but not to gain wealth. She had more important needs.

Bridget, daughter of a slave, dressed in coarse, brown sack cloth, appeared at the door of Duvah's large, sturdy log fortress.

A guard in leather armor met her at the gate, a huge wolfhound at his side. Looking at her shabby dress and bare feet, he demanded to know her purpose.

"I am the daughter of Brocessa, the slave, and Duvah, the prince of Leinster," she answered stoutly. "I will see Duvah and declare myself."

Puzzled at her bold confidence, the guard took her inside the gates, through the yard and into the big house. They found Duvah sitting at a long, oaken table having a meal with his wife. A feast sat before them. Light from tall, narrow windows gleamed on two golden candlesticks and the shining pewter plates and tankards. They were both dressed in the fine velvets and embroidery and furs of the gentry.

The guard announced the young girl beside him in her ragged, brown muslin, stating that she claimed to be daughter of the prince.

The wife of the prince, she who had cast the slave

woman out, was horrified and furious. Duvah, the prince father, seemed bemused.

"Are you then?" he asked, studying the amazing beauty of his child. "And how came you to be here?"

"So then, what have we to do with you?" the newly designated stepmother railed. "What do you want? Are you going to try to displace my own three children and take away their inheritance? Imposter! Faker! Thief! Where is your master? You are surely a runaway slave! Leave here before I set the hounds on you."

Duvah interrupted, "If you are the child of my wanderings, where then is your mother? Is she Brocessa, the slave? Has she died then?" He was curious about the little maid he once found enticing, a worthy lass for a night's game.

"She is not dead. Indeed she was a slave and so was I," was Bridget's crisp answer. "Now she rests from her burdensome labors in the Abbey of St. Francis, a free woman. Illan the Druid set us both free. As for me, I want to be acknowledged, that is all. I want my mother to be known as favored by a prince. I want to see the heritage I was born to. Then I will go."

"You will not go!" Duvah stood up, a tall, sturdy, handsome man with thick beard and hair the same tawny shade as Bridget's. "Gladly I will let the world know that this lovely lass is my child! You will stay here." He gave his wife a warning look. "You shall be treated like the princess you are. And I will find for you a husband worthy of your beauty and family."

"No. No husband."

Startled, Duvah looked at her sharply. "What are you saying?"

"I want no husband to lord over me. I have work to do for the Master. A husband would get in the way."

"What foolishness is this?" Duvah fumed. "Of course you will marry, and marry well! I'll see to that. Now settle yourself into your rightful home and prepare to be a joyful bride."

"I will be a bride," Bridget said quietly, *"but not to a mortal man."*

Then came suitors, fine young men, champions, chieftains, princes. They came for the grandest prize in all Ireland, a wealthy lass in the royal line who, above all, was the sweetest natured and most beautiful.

She turned them all down.

Her father was furious, and so was his wife after they had a private conversation. A good, well-made marriage contract could be a great asset. Alliances, lands, cattle, perhaps a new opportunity to claim the kingship of Leinster, all sorts of benefits could come to them through the factoring of his daughter.

But she continued to give to the poor anything of value that came to hand. If, riding in a wagon, she saw a wizened, old hag freezing along the side of the road, she gave her a luxurious fur robe to wrap in. If a poor man appeared at the door for a bite to eat, she gave him food and the golden plate upon which it was served.

Duvah, goaded by his wife, saw that Bridget was giving away everything they had. It appeared that they, too, could soon be begging beside the road!

She would not marry to their benefit. She was utterly generous with their property. Bridget was a millstone around their necks, pulling them and their children

down to ruin. Duvah began to harbor a deep fury for his newly found daughter. A princess she might be, but a fool of one, and a detriment to the House of Leinster!

One day, as Bridget walked among the gentle sheep in the meadow, Duvah pulled up in his chariot. He took her by the arm and propelled her to the wagon, where he heaved her unceremoniously into the back.

"Where are we going, Father?" Bridget asked.

"I will tell you where we are going!" he declared. "You give away every good thing we have. You refuse to marry even the finest of suitors. I am taking you to meet my kinsman, King Dunlaing MacEnda, the king of Leinster. This is not for your honor. I am going to ask him *to buy you* as a bondservant. With your beauty and your talent for farm work, you should bring a good price, which may repay me for some that you have stolen from me!"

Bridget felt her heart go heavy. She was not surprised at her father's plan. After all, she was the daughter of a bondswoman, and he had the right to do it. Nor was she afraid of the work, which she truly loved. But dismay filled her that she would not be able to do the service to the Master that she felt called to do.

She bowed her head as they bumped along on the road. "*So be it, Lord,*" she said in her heart, submitting to His mysterious and unyielding will.

They arrived at the gateway to the palace of Leinster. Tall, carved, wooden pillars flanked the entranceway.

Duvah let himself down from the chariot and started to enter the building. A guard in metal armor and helmet stopped him.

"I am Duvah, the prince of Leinster. I have come to

visit my kinsman," Duvah argued.

"If this is a friendly visit, you will have no use for that sword."

Reluctantly, Duvah unbuckled his scabbard and laid the sword and sheath on the seat of the chariot. He had hoped to impress the king with the expensive craftsmanship and heavily jeweled hilt of the weapon, but never mind. The thing of concern right now was to rid himself of a troublesome, young woman who apparently was his daughter.

After some time, Duvah and the king came through the gates, the father broadly extolling the beauty and virtues of the maiden he wanted to sell. As they approached the wagon, the king was already impressed with the striking loveliness of the offered product. Suddenly Duvah stopped cold.

"Where is my sword?"

"It was a leper, Father. The poor man was struggling along the road on a crutch, his rags hanging on his poor, starving body. I had to help him. I had nothing else. I gave him your sword."

Duvah was confounded. His eyes popped out in his purpling face.

"You gave away my jeweled sword? And to some old leper!"

"He needed food. He was about to die."

Duvah raised his hand to strike her. He wanted to beat her to death.

"Wait now, kinsman." The king took hold of his arm. "She will be no good to you maimed or killed. See here, lass. I cannot take you into my house. You would surely be even more generous with my goods than you are with your father's."

"Christ knows that I would indeed." She did not apologize. "If I had all the wealth that you possess I would give it to His poor."

Dunlaing turned to Duvah. "We have no right to buy or sell this lass. She belongs to the Lord God and His Son."

∽⊘∾

Bridget married. On February 1, 470 A.D. she gowned herself in a simple, white linen kirtle and bowed at the altar in the stone oratory of Bishop Usneach in West Meath and received the veil of the Bride of Christ.

Then she went to work, joyfully, vigorously, serving the poor, teaching the Word of God, setting up an abbey in Kildare where no one was ever turned away from food and shelter.

Country girl that she was, the nuns kept plenty of cattle, sheep, and cornfields to support their ministry to the poor. Often when they could not find their happy abbess, they had only to look out on the fields and meadows among the milch cows and sheep.

Holy men, searching for a sanctuary where they could both study the Scriptures and serve a useful life for Christ, came to Bridget, and a wing was built for their quarters.

Word came that there were many poor in Connaught, the stony west of Eire. Bridget left her monastery in Kildare and began works in many other places, building thirty more monasteries and schools.

Bridget was strong of body and will. Her heart was to the poor, but she was so stunningly beautiful that it was rumored that she prayed for disfigurement so that no one would want to divert her from the purpose that God had entrusted to her.

She never was disfigured. She remained as beautiful of face as she was of soul until the day she died and was buried beside that other icon of Irish faith, St. Patrick, in County Down.

Gormlaith of Clontarf

For nearly three hundred years, the Viking raiders had plundered Ireland, focusing principally on churches and monasteries. They settled in the town of Dublin because the River Liffey made a convenient avenue for their colorful ships to enter from the sea. Occasionally they married into Irish clans and became kings, but the terrible pillaging and murder continued. They were seldom seriously challenged because each of the Irish kings had more concern for his own little domain than for the good of the country as a whole.

Then came along the great Brian Boru, the son of Cinneide (Kennedy), a minor king. Boru forced the scattered armies together to fight one final, gigantic battle against the Norseland pirates, a war that was brought about by the selfish conniving of one vicious queen, Gormlaith.

Succaret, the Breton slave boy, lifted the heavy bar and threw open the wooden shutters of the northwest corner tower of the Viking palace in Dublin.

"Hurry, you lazy Gall, get them wider so that I can see the whole scene. Now get out of my way!" Gormlaith pushed him aside and leaned out of the casement.

"They are coming," she purred. "I can just barely see Brian Boru's ragtag army coming over yon rise from the west. Listen! Listen, Mora! Can you hear them singing the Rosg-Catha? What a pitiful crew of odd soldiers, their banners are all different colors and strange designs. Trees, of all the petty, feeble things, and dogs and harps. I catch only a glimpse of armor in this early light. They are wearing only tunics and leather. That will make easy work for my son Sitric's pirates and the Scots. Sitric said that Brian Boru has enlisted twenty thousand warriors from all over Ireland to fight against the Danes. Twenty-thousand! But they have absolutely no chance against our Vikings. We have more than that number. It will be the grandest of battles, and *all for me!*"

Behind her in the depths of the tower room came the quiet voice of Mora, Gormlaith's daughter-in-law. She sat on a pillow atop a heavy, wooden stool in the middle of the floor, her sewing spread out around her, her needles and thread piled in a basket at her side. Against the wall, two heavy and well-carved wooden chairs flanked a long table equally as elaborately decorated, attesting to the fine craftsmanship of the Danes. On the table, sat a beautiful silver pitcher full of fresh, cold water and two silver beakers, waiting for any sudden thirst of Mora's while busying herself in her handi-

work room. On the table, also, were two tall, magnificent golden candlesticks, the designs molded into their stems of the Cross and saints' faces were no doubt created by the skills of murdered Christian monks in some ravaged monastery.

"Indeed. It is so that you are partly responsible for this war." The younger woman raised her head to stare angrily at her mother-in-law. The early sunlight from the window brightened her auburn hair. "Many a valiant Irishman will die because you persuaded my husband to raise an army in an effort to finally conquer Ireland for the Danes. Were it not for Ospak, Brodar's henchman, slipping around to bring word to Brian Boru of this alliance between Sigurd of Northumbria and Brodar, the pirate, and your son, King Sitric of Dublin, Ireland would have been caught off guard at this invasion. My father had time to gather warriors and prepare for battle."

"*I did that!* I planned this grand battle and I am glad." Gormlaith stood up tall and proud, a flowing, saffron gown draped over her fine figure and a purple cloak pinned at her shoulder with a jeweled brooch. Chains of gold glittered in the braids of her rich, red hair, which was wrapped around her haughty head. "No one, not in Ireland or Lochlin or Brittany could have changed the hatred of these two kings into allies, no one but myself. Your father, Brian Boru, will regret the day he sent me away, his wife. And King Malachy, also! Another fool of a king who did not realize my power when he married me. Who would believe that Brian, king of Connaught, and Malachy, the king of Tara, would be forced to become allies because of me? It's delicious! They will learn that I will not be despised."

The mother of a grown man, Sitric Silkenbeard, the chief of the Vikings in Dublin, Gormlaith ni Flahertie, was still the most breathtakingly beautiful woman in Ireland. Her skin was alabaster, with just a tinge of rose. No wonder, it was, that three kings fawned over her, proudly married her and then, as witnessed by her avaricious green eyes, found her impossible to live with.

"The Irish warriors are singing the Rosg-Catha. I could hear them singing, twenty thousand voices, as they left Kilmainham before daylight. Let them sing. Let them play the pipes. Brian Boru will die today!"

"I believe it's only revenge you're wanting on my father for divorcing you. And Malachy, too. Even Sitric's poor old father, Aulaf, king of the Vikings, couldn't bear you and hid himself in a monastery until he died. With Malachy, you were queen of Tara, and with my father, Brian Boru MacKennedy, you were queen of Cashel, and they both cast you and your evil conspiracies aside."

"Watch your tongue!" Gormlaith turned on the younger woman like a harpy. "I will tell my son of your insolence, and he will have your head on a pike!"

Mora continued to sit quietly, her head bent over her sewing. The venom of her mother-in-law and Sitric's pliability in his mother's hands were not new to her. In the few years since Brian Boru had given his daughter in marriage to the Viking chief, Mora O'Brien had suffered so many threats that she almost wished they would follow through and cease her misery. In his advanced age, Brian had himself married Gormlaith in an effort to cement peace between the Viking settlers and the natural Celtic Irish. He found it an impossible alliance.

It was agony Mora felt about the danger to her father and the terrible battle to come today, on Good Friday, 1014. She knew her father had tried to hold the battle off to a day other than the holy day of Christ's sacrifice, but superstitious Brodar had it from the Danish rune stones that only on a Friday would he succeed.

By leaning far out the window, Gormlaith could see the head of the Viking forces tramping across the fields from Clontarf on the northeast of Dublin, where their strange, colorful longships lay at anchor in Dublin Bay. Powerful, strong voices chanted the skalds in time to the beat of their marching feet. Soon the woman caught sight of the Viking banners, crimson flags all, with striking black ravens. "Ah, now, there's an army!"

Mora knew her aging father was out there, across the Liffey bogland from where she sat in the Dublin fortress, rallying his troops around the Cross, reminding them of the constant ransacking, devastation, and murders of Irish people and the burning of Christian holy places by the heathen Viking pirates. Mora's brothers would be there, too, Murrogh and Donal, Teige and Donogh, Conor and Flann. How she feared for them, fine warriors though they were, in the certain danger of the Norsemen's battle axes.

Gormlaith continued to lean far out of the window, holding her breath, waiting.

"The trumpets sound. The pipes are skirling. It begins!" she shouted in ecstasy. "They are screaming battle cries! Oh, the clang of swords and armor! Brian and Malachy have no chance against the iron armor and helmets of the men of my brother, Molloy, and my son, Sitric. Those ignorant Irish are wearing almost no armor. Come and see!"

"I have no wish to see." Mora's voice raised in anguish. "I take no pleasure in watching men slice and bash one another and splatter blood. I think you misjudge the spirit of our Irish army, Gormlaith. For too many long years we have lived in dread of the raiders from the north, killing our priests, stealing treasures from the churches and monasteries, carrying off our children for slaves. You have pushed their fury to the breaking point. We now have the opportunity to end all of that forever. The Irish love for their country and Brian Boru will give them uncanny strength and power and unity that they never had before. You will see!"

"*Power!* What do you know of power, you silly girl. I have tasted power. I pull the strings of kings like puppets, and they dance for me, even when they don't know they are doing it. When Sitric and Molloy come back victorious today, I will be high queen of all Ireland!"

"And myself?" Mora asked. "As Sitric's wife, I am queen of Dublin. Would I not be queen of their conquered lands? It is a role I do not want, but what of me?"

Gormlaith turned away from the window, her green eyes narrowed like a cat watching her prey. "Oh, I have plans for you, my girl. Brian Boru's daughter will receive rewards worthy of her haughty, stubborn father. As for myself, I have been promised to Brodar, the Viking pirate king."

"And Sigurd, the Scotsman, also."

A derisive laugh burst from the woman's red lips. "Ah yes, my son does get carried away, promising the greatest prize to anyone when it is necessary to raise an army. But Sigurd is clumsy. Likely he will be killed. If not, then wouldn't it be grand sport if they had to battle, one on one, for my hand? How I would love that! I would become legendary. If Sigurd won, I can handle him quite easily. But Brodar! *Now there's a man!* Big as a tree, powerful, mysterious. What a match for me. What a pair we would make!"

Mora shuddered over her sewing. "He frightens me. Those piercing brown eyes. And that bush of black hair so long that he tucks it into his belt. The man worships Satan and Bel and demons, not the true God. I fear him. And so should you be wary of him, Gormlaith ni Flahertie."

"Fear him?" Gormlaith sneered. "I think not! It's proud I would be to bed that grand man and share his throne over Ireland." She turned back to the window.

Sounds of raging battle of thousands of warriors roared into the room and echoed off its walls, the clang of iron broadswords, the screams of men as thick spears pierced through their bodies and bright red blood burst out, the crushing clunk of battle axes as they split helmets and chopped skulls. The noise filled the room until Mora felt it was smothering her. She wanted to cover her ears and run away. But she must not let Gormlaith's taunting keep her from following the course of the war. Her family was out there among the forty thousand men determined to kill and maim and butcher one another.

Mora's fingers shook hard as she tried desperately to

sew, to do something positive instead of listening to the bloody horror that went on only half a mile away in front of Dublin Castle. She blinked tears and squinted her eyes, trying to see the linen fabric of a kirtle she was making for herself. All she could see in her mind was her father and brothers being slaughtered. Every scream sounded like one of her kin. Even her nephew, Torlogh, Murrogh's son, was involved in the havoc.

"Why do you sit there and sew?" raged Gormlaith. "History is being made before our eyes. As far as I can see there are warriors and flying weapons. It's grand! Come and see! I don't know why you sew anyway. There are plenty of slaves to do it for you. I cannot bear such drudgery. My brother, Molloy, once had the gall to ask me to sew a button for him. It was a time when I was married to your father and living at Kincora Castle near the Shannon. Molloy was bringing a load of three ship's masts that he had contracted to sell to Brian. He was wearing a fancy, blue tunic given to him by Brian. The load of poles slipped and caught Molloy's shirt and ripped off a silver button. 'Sister,' he said to me as I descended the staircase when he arrived. 'Sister, come and sew on this button. This is a fine shirt and I don't wish to allow Brian to see how I damaged it.' Worried, he was, about how Brian would become offended. How dare he ask me, the queen of Cashel and Connaught, to sew a shirt!"

For a second, Mora ignored the clash of battle and responded, "I see nothing wrong with that. If a mistress does not know how to sew, then how will she know if her slaves are doing a good job of it? My mother, the only wife my father had before you, the mother of all my brothers and myself, she taught me these things."

"You would not understand," Gormlaith sneered. "You are not fit to be a queen. I scolded and shamed my brother for accepting petty gifts from that old man. I made him realize how stupid he looked. By the time I got through with him, he was brought so low that he was ashamed and furious with himself for being so timid. I threw the shirt in the fire, and he did not object. He looked foolish."

"My father would not see it so." Mora stopped sewing and gazed at the open window. From her view, sitting on the stool, all she could see was a sky whitened with clouds, a deeper gray bank rising in the northwest. Then a sudden wind gusted through the casement, and with it came the warm smell of blood. The scent of the gory throng, hacked and sliced raw, blew across the bogland and filled the air in the room.

Mora went white. Nausea flooded over her. Her brain whirled.

"Smelling it, aren't you? The blood!" Gormlaith tormented the younger woman. "Does it not thrill you? Does it not make you want to take up sword and charge out into the battle like a Danish Valkyrie? Come, you spineless female, let me make you angry enough to fight. I did that for my brother. On the same day of the button, I shamed him so that, when he advised your brother, Murrogh, to make a certain move in a chess game with his cousin, Conang, and Murrogh lost the game and blamed it on Molloy, he was furious. Murrogh insulted him and said it was Molloy's bad advice that lost Molloy the battle of Glen Mama, too. Molloy was ready to kill. He left the castle and, when

Brian sent a lackey after him with offers of peace and more gifts, Molloy cracked the servant's skull and tossed him into the river. Ah!" Gormlaith glanced out the window. "Is that Brian Boru in the thick of the battle?"

Instantly Mora dropped her sewing and rushed to the opening. "Where? Where do you see my father?"

Gormlaith laughed. "Oh, 'tis only a brother of yours. Which one?"

It was impossible to tell. Mora could not even discern which warrior Gormlaith thought was her relative. All she could see was a mass of bodies twisted together all over the ground. Other bodies covered with blood charged over the wounded and dead, waving sword and axe to bring down more to the heaps of bloody, wasted lives.

Desperately, Mora searched for signs of her family, but they all looked alike. She could barely tell which men wore armor and which did not, the gore was so thick. A cloud hung over the battlefield, not a healthy rain cloud, but an ugly, gray fog of dust and heaving breaths and shattered iron.

A rider came running hard over the double ramparts and clattered across the bridge toward the castle gateposts.

"You there!" Gormlaith called out. "How goes the battle?"

The horseman pulled his animal up short. "Who asks?" he demanded. "Ah, it is you, Mistress. And the little queen. The battle goes on. I can see no victor at all. Our Vikings are champions, but the Irish are in a fury to beat the Danes out of Ireland. It's a terrible time of savage blood, it is."

"My father," Mora called down. "Have you seen him?"

"Not at all. We're thinking the Irish have secreted him somewhere for his safety, the old man not able to stand and fight any more. But your brothers, I saw two of them fall already."

"Two of my brothers," Mora wept. "Which two?"

But the rider had already urged his horse and went through the arched gateway into the courtyard calling for fresh supplies for the fight.

"No victor yet," Gormlaith mused. She stayed at the window, watching, listening, waiting for word to come that the ferocious Vikings had killed her enemies, her former husbands who despised her.

On and on it went, through the long Irish day and into the deepening twilight, the dreadful clamor of a multitude of warriors.

Mora came and went from the tower chamber, trying to busy herself, tears brimming in her blue eyes. Time after time she knelt in her own apartment before the Cross, pleading with the saints for the lives of her family, begging for victory for the Christians who defended their land and people.

"He comes!" Gormlaith cried out at last, exulting. "My son, my victor, he comes!"

Looking out, Mora saw her husband, King Sitric Silkenbeard, riding hard across the space between the wall of fence pales and the palace, his blonde hair flying without a helmet, his tunic soaked with blood, and his coat of mail in shreds.

The women rushed down the staircase from the tower in time to see him stumble through the doors.

"Sitric, are you wounded?" Mora cried.

Panting, he fell onto the bottom steps and lay back, exhausted. The slave Succaret rushed to him with a mug of water. He gulped it down and sent for more.

"Tell me!" shouted Gormlaith, leaning over him, demanding. "How is the battle going?"

He tore off the remnants of his armor and ripped at the blood-saturated tunic while he gasped, "I am not wounded to death. But it is over. The battle is done."

"Then we are the victors," she smiled triumphantly.

"No, no! We are defeated. The Irish fought like demons. I thought that Malachy was not going to fight, but he waited until the last and brought his fresh men into the battle. So many dead. Sigurd and the Scots and Danes. Thousands of them ran to the seashore. But the ships, the Viking longboats, were being pushed out to sea by the wind. And suddenly a terrible wave roared over the beach. They drowned! Thousands!"

Mora fell to her knees beside him, hands clasped in thankfulness for the miracle. Then she asked, "My father, Brian Boru, and my brothers . . . ?"

"Murrogh is dead. I saw him fall. And Teige and Conor. Donal has taken the lead of the Irish army. Brian has not been seen since he rallied the troops this morning. I'm sure his soldiers have the old man tucked away and guarded somewhere. Listen to me," he said, still breathing hard, facing Mora, eyes watering and wild with fear, his face red and sweating hard. "When they come for me, and it's sure that they will, to torture me and take my head, you must plead with them for my life, do you hear me, Mora, my wife?"

Before Mora could answer, Gormlaith broke in hastily, "My brother, Molloy . . . ?"

"Dead."

"And Brodar? Where is he?"

"I saw him running into the woods when the retreat began."

Mora, tears streaming down her cheeks for her dead brothers, quickly called for water and cloths to wipe away the blood, and she stripped the torn tunic off Sitric. There was a gash across his stomach just below his ribs, but not deep enough to expose his vitals. She ordered wine and bread and meat to be readied for him, and bound his body with linen.

Gormlaith stalked back and forth in a fury, long-nailed fingers tearing at her clothes.

"This cannot be! We had more warriors, professional men of war. How could this happen?" She turned to her son. "How could you let this happen? You are a weakling like your father, an ignorant, sniveling creature. You must find Brodar. *He is a man.* He will do something to turn it around."

Suddenly Sitric raised up, hunched over his dreadful wound, shaking, one hand braced against the wall. He faced his ranting mother and, for the first time in his life, he shouted at her.

"You! You selfish, greedy old woman! My friends are all killed. If I hadn't run away, I would have been sliced to pieces by now. Leave my sight, you evil harpy. For you, the Plain of Dublin and the bog lies in blood. Blood drips off the trees. Leave me!"

For a second, Gormlaith looked stunned. Then those green eyes flashed fire and narrowed.

"I will leave, and you will find that I am a deadly enemy, Sitric Silkenbeard. I will go to Brodar. We will make this a victory!"

She wrapped her cloak close around her and sent Succaret for a horse and chariot. Swiftly she was out of the big, oaken castle and gone.

It was late and dark when Mora heard the sound of hooves outside the doors. Succaret and a tired guard went out to see and came back, carrying Gormlaith in their arms. The woman's face was gray-white, her eyes staring. She trembled.

Mora hurried the man to carry Gormlaith to the woman's bed chamber and sent for wine. Sitric was in his bed, surfeited with wine to kill the pain of his wound and allow him to sleep.

"Gormlaith, where have you been? What have you seen? My father, Brian Boru, did you see him? Does he live?"

Gormlaith's cat eyes grew pleased and she smiled the most evil smile. "He is dead. His head lifted from his shoulders by Brodar, the Giant."

Mora laid her head on the bedpost, weeping.

"But Brodar, the Great One, he no longer lives." Gormlaith lay back on the cushions and frowned, as if puzzled that her schemes could have gone so awry. "Brian's men caught him and they . . ." Her eyes widened as if seeing something too horrible to describe. Then her eyelids closed. "I have to think. I have to plan. The Vikings are defeated. I must find a new king, a new champion."

Even as Mora watched, incredible, beautiful Gormlaith lay on the pillows, pale, disheveled, the flesh on her white skin shrinking , fading . . . a very old woman.

With King Brian Boru gone, the only king who was able to draw together all of Ireland to drive out their common enemy, the island slipped back into scattered, petty kingdoms at war with one another. Brian had given permission for peaceful Danish traders to remain in their cities of commerce, Wexford, Waterford, and Limerick.

Gormlaith was sent to live in Mellicourt convent and died there.

Dearvorgilla, the Unforgettable

After the defeat of the Viking raiders, Ireland settled down for about a hundred years with no troubles greater than the normal bloody little battles among the kings. In the year 1155, Pope Adrian IV "gave" Ireland to King Henry II of England for "checking their descent into wickedness . . . and encouraging the growth of faith of Christ." This, to the only country of Europe that was unaffected by the fall of Rome and had sent priests and teachers to salvage civilization on the Continent. King Henry couldn't care less about that primitive island, and so he ignored His Holiness's edict.

Then, one day, the usurper of the kingship of Leinster "abducted" the wife of the king of Breffni.

illie, my dear love, come and share my pillow tonight."

King Tiernan O'Rourke winked his one good eye at his lovely wife and smoothed his graying mustache playfully.

Dearvorgilla's countenance drooped and she bowed her head, letting her silky, golden hair fall around her face. Her red lips drew into a troubled, trembling rosebud.

"I cannot. Oh, my dear husband, I fear I may never share our marriage bed again. I am so distressed."

Alarm widened O'Rourke's eye. "What are you talking about? You are my wife and you will come to my bed whenever I please!"

The woman turned her back, head hung down in sorrow, gazing out the window of the castle toward the high, blue mountain. "How can I, my lord? I would lie beside you in agony knowing that you are sure to burn in the fires of Hell while I shall someday delight in the joys of Heaven. As I listened to the oratory this morning, I realized this sorrowful fact. You have been evil. Evil, evil! While I have been faithful in my prayers and attending mass. I have lighted candles for you, but you have never repented of your deeds. Someday soon you may die, but when I go to Heaven, I will not find my beloved husband there!"

O'Rourke smiled indulgently. "Why, my dear queen, I will go to mass with you tomorrow, that I will. I will say prayers of penance, if such prayers are needed. I had no idea you worried about my soul. Such sweet concern for me."

"To mass? *Only to mass?* Oh, my husband, your sins

are too great to find forgiveness at a simple mass."

"Why, my dear, what have I done to deserve the fires of Hell?"

"Sure then, are you so cold that you do not remember when you attacked the monastery at Tullaghard? The monks and servants rushed to the tower out of fear, and you set a fire in the entrance. It blazed up throughout the wooden steps and floors inside, and they were horribly killed. Don't you remember?"

"Well I remember, sure, quite well I do. I attacked Tullaghard because their king raided my herds."

"But those poor people in the tower were innocents. My heart breaks for them. And now it must break for you. You have earned the flames of Purgatory."

"What can I do, Gillie my lovely rose, to set your mind at ease?" O'Rourke caressed her, feeling the firm, warm flesh of her young body in a silk robe under his hand. More than ever he was determined to take her to his connubial bed.

"You must go to Lough Dearg. There at St. Patrick's Purgatory, you must fast and meditate and do penance for three days, as other contrite pilgrims do. You must pray and pray for cleansing from your awful sins." Dearvorgilla's wide blue eyes glistened with tears. "Then, you will come back to me and our marriage will be holy and full of delights again."

"Very well. I will do it. I will do it tomorrow. But tonight . . ."

She drew back from his touch. "Tonight I must stay in my own chamber. I will be on my knees before the shrine praying for you all night so that we will soon be united as one body again."

"One body." How well his wife knew the words that stirred his aging blood to race, that made him feel her scented and soft flesh against his. Sure then, he could force her to come to his bed, but he knew from past experience that all he would receive for his stubborn persistence was a cold, rigid, and unwilling female with no warmth or pliable responses.

Very well, he would go to Lough Dearg. He would camp on the island and listen to the chanting admonitions of the monks, and visit the cave where Saint Patrick had seen a vision of the fiery mouth of Hell, and go through the motions of penitence for his sins, whatever they may be.

In truth he really didn't think he had much to be penitent about. It was not uncommon for kings in Ireland to war against one another and destroy the properties and people of their enemies. The tower at Tullaghard adjoined the monastery there. The people were subjects to a rival king. All enemies must be destroyed, peasants, priests, warriors, and kings alike. That was war.

Nevertheless, he would go, with the delicious anticipation of the vibrant joys, honeymoon of days and nights, he would receive when his sweet Dearvorgilla welcomed home her cleansed and Heaven-bound husband.

The next morning early, Queen Dearvorgilla watched from an upper window as Tiernan O'Rourke and several companions rode through the gates of Breffni Castle on their way to Lough Dearg and the island, a good ninety miles south of Breffni. Three days travel, three days penance walking barefoot on the sharp rocks of the island, and three days coming home. That would be enough.

Calling her maid, Bridey, she handed her a flowered twig from a Maybush. With a secretive smile, she said, "Take this to Tomas in the stable."

Shortly she saw the groom leave the castle yard and ride into the forest eastward.

For two days, Dearvorgilla lazed about the castle, frequently staring out the window, nervously pecking at some embroidery, only nibbling her meals.

"Why, Mistress," Bridey ventured. "Why are you agitated? Have some wine. Rest yourself."

The queen looked at her sharply, then let her eyelids droop. "Why then should I not be solemn and anxious? My good husband has taken a journey at my bidding. It is a long way to Lough Dearg. He took only a few warriors with him. He may be set upon by murdering thieves. Or he may be attacked while going through the territory of another king. I could never forgive myself if he is lost to me. But neither can I bear the thought of him burning in Hell without forgiveness while I delight in the presence of Christ. Leave me, Bridey. I must go to my knees before the cross for him again."

As the days stretched on, Dearvorgilla became more and more distressed. Bridey did not again try to sooth her or ask why she was upset. It would be only a couple more days and King Tiernan O'Rourke would be home again and calm her fears.

Finally, one evening, the queen asked her, "Tomas. Did he ever come back from his errand?"

"Errand? Oh, the sending of him out with the

Maybush flower. Why, I believe not, Mistress."

Dearvorgilla slammed her golden plate onto the table, scattering fruit to the floor. "Why has he not come? It was only a simple errand that I sent him to do!"

"Shall we send someone to find him?"

"No! No, no. I will be patient," the queen said, but she marched across the floor and slammed the heavy, wooden door of her chamber behind her.

"She'll be going to the shrine again, poor thing," Bridey said aloud, and the servants in the room nodded sympathetically.

All was quiet in the darkness of the next night, when suddenly a band of horsemen came galloping into the castle courtyard. They killed the two guards at the gates and leaped off their horses, bursting through the huge castle doors with shouts and flaming torches. The servants ran to hide from the wild invaders.

Slashing cushions, dumping over tables and chairs, setting fire to portiers and grabbing every valuable utensil they saw, the ravaging intruders pillaged the entry hall. Then they rushed up the steps to the upper floor. One of them kicked in the door of Queen Dearvorgilla's chamber!

Bridey and her fellows heard her scream! The raider scooped her into his arms and strode out and down the stairs, she calling for help all the way while the household attendants watched, terrified, from their hiding places. Out the castle door the raiders went, Dearvorgilla still screaming for help.

The marauders left as they came, carrying with them golden cups and jewelry and even the royal torque. Riding in front of the leader on his horse was the wife of King Tiernan O'Rourke!

"Did you see?" a lackey shouted. "The queen had barely enough time to catch up her cloak when he took her."

"At least she will have her cover against the night cold," Bridey said. "Clearly, she has been up all night worrying about her sire. She was still fully dressed."

Only the next day, O'Rourke came riding into his fortress anticipating the joyful and relieved welcome waiting for him. After the rigors of his pilgrimage on the island of Lough Dearg, he felt ready to take his wife thoroughly and then go out and enjoy more sin against his foes.

He was stunned when he heard of the raid and that his beautiful, saintly queen had been abducted!

"Who was it?" he demanded of the servants. "Who dared to lay hands on the wife of The O'Rourke?"

Tomas, the groom, stepped forward. "It was King Dermott MacMurrough," he swore. "I remember seeing him at the council of Tara. There were kings there from Meath and Munster and Connaught, and MacMurrough from Ferns by Wexford. I saw him, and it's sure he set his sights on Queen Dearvorgilla from that time."

Newly cleansed, Tiernan O'Rourke began a new list of sins, with various graphic descriptions of his intentions for MacMurrough, the kidnapper.

"Mount your horses!" he shouted. "We will bring back my queen!"

Bridey, the maid, stepped forward. "Oh, be careful, my king," she cautioned. "Remember, MacMurrough murdered King Don MacLochlainn to make himself king of Leinster. He is a vicious brute of a man. Many a monastery he has burned, many a town he has destroyed, trying to take more territory for himself. It is said that he hired a churlish soldier to rape the abbess of Kildare in order to appoint his own relative in her place. He may be prepared to murder you. He has an army, and he will expect a fine man such as you to come for your queen. You must be prepared for battle."

Shaking with frustration and fury, O'Rourke's one good eye blazed, but he recognized with amazing swiftness the wisdom in the little maid's advice.

"So I must," he ranted. "Oh, the horror of it! That my saintly wife should be violated by a beast like Dermott MacMurrough. But I will save her, I will! Send word to the high king! Rory O'Connor will bring his army and go with me to rescue her!"

King Rory O'Connor was more than willing to help O'Rourke battle the despicable Dermott MacMurrough. Everyone in Ireland seemed to hate the man for his vicious, devastating raids on churches and towns. He had declared himself king of all of Leinster, the east side of the island, and was determined to make it happen if he had to kill every peasant and monk and monarch he found. Instead of gaining ground, he was losing it. O'Connor had pushed him back until he had only a small piece of Wexford area and his headquarters at Ferns.

It took almost a year for Rory O'Connor to gather his troops. If Dearvorgilla was worried about her husband suffering Hell's pangs, she would have been satisfied to see his agonies during that time. The nights he raged in his bed, imagining that brute MacMurrough enjoying his wife's endowments and her sweet spiritual tenderness. The days he spent riding, practicing with sword and sling the things he would do to the abductor. His warriors rode with him, admiring the old fellow's tenacity.

O'Connor called an assemblage of all the chiefs and kings. At the castle in Dublin, they came together to discuss what must be done about Dermott MacMurrough and his despicable lawlessness and cruelty. Many of the kings complained of the offenses MacMurrough performed in Ireland. Abducting another king's wife was the final outrage.

In the grand hall with its tall pillars and heavy, wooden furnishings, the kings drank their mead and leaned back on the thrones, tossing aside their constricting fur robes. The atmosphere became more and more filled with uncontrollable fury.

MacMurrough's father was there, eyes full of anger at the foul words describing his son. O'Rourke took the floor and raged about the brutish criminal who had taken his wife. The elder MacMurrough kept quiet, watching his ravings, but finally leaned over to a neighbor and murmured a remark, wondering if the lady had not been delighted to be kidnapped from such an old horse as O'Rourke.

In a flash, O'Rourke grabbed a shillelagh and crushed the old man's head. He was killed.

The men in the room were so inflamed with fury that they felt no remorse for the death of a man who had raised such a depraved outlaw.

"We would do the same for Dermott if he were here. What shall we do with the body?"

"Send his head to Dermott."

"Hang his body to rot on the road to Wexford."

"Let's not bother with such time-consuming chores. We'll bury the man right here in the assembly room as an example to others who insult women and encourage crime."

The hole was dug in the middle of the earthen floor. O'Rourke had left the room and came back through the door with the bloody body of a stinking, mangy mongrel dog. He tossed the dog's body into the grave along with the elder MacMurrough.

"Two of a kind," he said.

They filled the hole. The Assembly settled down to finish their work. Without much discussion, they decided to run Dermott MacMurrough off his lands and take away his kingship. Every king offered troops to insurrect his dwelling at Ferns, rescue Queen Dearvorgilla O'Rourke, and drive him into the wilderness.

At Ferns, Dermott MacMurrough received word that he was about to be dethroned and possibly beheaded by a massive effort of the kings of Ireland. He began to prepare his army to defend his property; however, at the same time, he had all his gold gathered up ready to carry away with him. He entered into a salon where Dearvorgilla sat savoring a cup of wine.

"Well now, my illicit love, our time of delights is coming to an end."

"Is it then? Where shall we go?"

"Not where shall *we* go, my lady, where shall *I* go? I will head for Connaught. I intend to hide in the mountains but, if I am found out, it's England for me. I will get support from King Henry. He will be glad to hear that I can gain control of Ireland for him. All I need is an English army behind me. Those Normans have grand equipment for winning battles against barbarians like our Celts."

"And what of me?" Dearvorgilla's blue eyes questioned. "You promised me riches and power."

"Why, my dear, you will go back to your fine Christian husband with his one eye and gray hairs. I know quite well that it was not riches you came with me to get. You were simply bored with the old fellow. We have had a frolic. It is over. Play the abused woman and he will take you back. As for me, I'm off to battle, behind the lines, of course. Goodbye to you, Dearvorgilla ni Melaghlin O'Rourke!"

He was gone. Dearvorgilla slammed the pewter cup against the closed door, splattering red liquid on the wall and floor. What of me? Dermott cares not. *Suicide?* No. *Run away?* To what? Another affair with another rascal chief? No.

Very well then. She knew it would come to an end. She could handle O'Rourke. He would pity her and come groveling to her for making her wait so long to be saved. The interlude was over.

For several days the battle raged, coming ever nearer to Ferns and the stone fortress. At last, Tiernan O'Rourke burst into the chamber where she sat waiting for him. Her heavy, carved chair was piled with colorful, soft cushions. The kirtle she wore was broidered with silken threads. A gold chain with a heavy medallion hung about her neck and lay on her bosom. Her silky, blonde hair was coiled to the top of her head with jeweled combs. The wine chalice was in her hand, filled.

She jumped up from her seat and rushed toward him. "Oh, my husband, my good husband! I have waited so long. Why did you not come sooner?"

Startled, O'Rourke stepped back. Dearvorgilla did not appear to be abused and neglected.

"My wife! My precious Gillie. What has happened to you? Have you been cruelly used? Oh my love, I am so sorry to have been so long coming to take you home with me!"

She sighed. "It has been a horrible ordeal. The coarseness of the man. Unspeakable! I shall be happy to go home to your bed, my dear husband."

Tiernan O'Rourke frowned, studying his wife while she finished the dregs of wine in the golden cup. She did not look desperate, tormented, suffering. Nevertheless, he would carry her back to Breffni.

"I only wish I could get my hands on Dermott MacMurrough!" O'Rourke said. "He would be cut into pieces and fed to the wild boars!"

"He is gone then?"

"He is. His army has lost touch with him. With no one to pay them, they have turned against him and run him into the wilderness. We will not see any more of him, I'm sure!"

Dearvorgilla was not so sure. "He has gone to King Henry, the king of England, to try to enlist his aid. He said the Normans would help him."

O'Rourke snorted. "A lot of good it will do him. He has nothing to bargain with, nothing to offer them. The land he murdered to steal, whatever booty he has taken from the people, all of it is gone, as he deserves."

"Well then, we may forget all about him. Likely

Ireland will never hear of him again. This episode is past and will never matter to anyone hereafter. You and I are together again."

As he took her hand to escort his lady down the steps of the castle at Ferns, a strange feeling of displeasure troubled the waters of Tiernan O'Rourke's soul. When he had her back at Breffni, there would be some interesting questions to answer.

When Dearvorgilla entered her own chamber in the castle at Breffni, Bridey waited for her, wearing a conspiratorial smile.

"Now then, my queen, was the delay long enough?" the little maid murmured.

The queen smiled with amusement. "Oh indeed it was. What an escapade. I was wined and dined and smothered with gifts. See here." She opened her cloak to show the young woman the magnificent jeweled medallion. "Ah, the nights were exquisite. Dermott treated me like the queen that I am, right up until King Tiernan came to 'rescue' me. It was grand!"

The little maid laughed with her mistress as they settled her into her home once more. "Just the lark you needed to break the boredom here at Breffni!"

Dearvorgilla fell onto a lounging chair and threw her arms wide. "Exactly. And what harm did it do? In a very short time, everyone will forget about it."

~◇~

Ireland never forgot.

Thirteen years later, Dermott MacMurrough traded his own daughter, Eva, and many grand promises to one Sir Richard de Clare, nicknamed Strongbow, in exchange for an army to regain Dermott's lands. Norman warriors came from Britain at MacMurrough's invitation to invade Ireland. Wexford and Waterford were destroyed, and the invaders, armed with more effective weapons and battle experience than the Celts, took over the whole of Eirinn, making serfs of the people. MacMurrough never did regain his kingship.

Ireland has never forgotten Dermott MacMurrough and Dearvorgilla, for their selfish indulgence broke open the door to the English invasion and Ireland's bloody, hungry, and destitute history through eight hundred long years.

King Tiernan O'Rourke sent his wandering wife to live until she died forty-six years later in the Abbey at Mellifont.

Grace O'Malley, the Pirate Queen

*England finally did take control of Ireland.
Four hundred years later, Elizabeth I became
queen of England and took pains to cash in
on Ireland's resources. She stripped the land
of its wonderful shillelagh oak trees to build
ships to fight the Spanish Armada. She demanded tribute from the Irish kings. And she
sent deputies into Ireland to bleed the land
and the people.*

Pull those oars, you lazy bulls! Steady now. Keep it
even until we pass the rocks. The tide's helping! Ho,
now! Someone's out of order. You there, Marty
MacDuffy. Pick up that oar and drop it in rhythm or I'll
have the hide off your back!"

The burly oarsman grinned behind his beard at his
captain, watching her stride down the deck, her leather
pampootie boots thumping briskly on the boards, the
wind catching her fiery red hair and blowing it around
her ruddy cheeks, her purple cloak with royal yellow lining billowing in the gusts. Her steps were heavier these

days with the weight of the grand bulge of her stomach. With powerful arms, Marty drew the oar against the water, synchronizing his strokes with his shipmates, trying to figure just how long it had been since the crew of the ship noticed her middle start to swell. Soon it should be that she would be birthing. It could happen right here on the ship. What a grand thing for her seamen to share!

Little fear he had that Grace O'Malley would scourge him. Seldom had there been a whipping in the ten years she ruled the waves around Clew Bay. There was no need. Her shouts, her foul and colorful words, the barking threats she made as she stood at the bowsprit with her red hair flying in the sea gales, endeared her to the rough sailors. She was a delight to be around and no fool, she. Born to the waves, she was. Her Da and his fathers for three centuries had ruled the waters around the west side of Ireland. Give her a sea battle or a land raid and her contagious enthusiasm for the fight and clever maneuverings were certain to bring them out proud and victorious.

She was an O'Malley, raised on the churning, heaving waters on the coast of Connaught. The O'Malley reputation—"invincible on land and sea!"—surpassed all others as mariners of the harsh Atlantic. When her father, Owen Ui Maile, died, he had no son of age so Grainne, called Grace, took over his fleet of galleys. She was wed to Donal O'Flaherty when she was fifteen years old. Bore him two sons and a daughter. Donal died in an accident and she sailed the sea.

Her ships waylaid and plundered Spanish trading ships passing Clare Island, her own domain. They

collected tolls from every vessel that came within thirty miles of the coast of Connaught, even French smugglers. Full bellies and plenty of French brandy and booty kept the sailors satisfied and loyal.

Grace stood at the prow, watching for rocks under the rippling white manes in the familiar harbor of Clew Bay. The galley ship moved away from Clare Island and out into the Atlantic. As soon as they were past the rocky coast where breakers relentlessly burst white spray against black rocks, then Grace shouted for the sails. Soon the grand, yellowed sheets ballooned overhead and the wind carried the ship out into the ocean.

This was no ordinary sailing. She would have to hold back her urge to go after every craft that entered her waters. There was no time for dallying with cargo and persecuting the captive crews after boarding a foreign ship. No, they must move along swiftly. They had been summoned to see the queen of England.

However, if they had any interference, Grace was ready for it. Likely, the English ships would give her plenty of space, for surely Elizabeth, the queen, would have alerted her vessels to avoid conflict with a ship flying the O'Malley seahorse and the lion of the O'Flahertys. Grace felt she had the right to display the proud O'Flaherty flag since her present husband was a nephew of her first spouse and Grace was considered a princess of the clan.

Looking far back toward the coast of Connaught, she could still make out the tall, square shape of Carrickhooley Castle standing almost in the water on a small peninsula. Two of her other ships were safely moored at Clare Island, tucked out of sight behind the wall of the tower house, cables running from their bows through a small aperture in the wall and directly into her bedroom. While she was there, no movement was made on her ships of which she was unaware. She was pleased with that stronghold.

They shipped the oars and let the magnificent tri-cornered sheets carry them as they sailed past Dingle and Kerry. After a day or two, they sighted on the south of Ireland, Cork Harbor and then the coast of Waterford. The sailors could sight land all along the southern coast of Munster. The crew began to wonder why they were not putting out to sea where they might snag an overstuffed Dutch tub or a careless English ship. Then they heard Grace and her present husband, Richard de Burgh, arguing, and they realized the older man was fretting about the infant soon to be born.

"Grannuelle, my love, we must be ready to beach immediately should you begin birth pangs!" Richard fussed plaintively. "That is my son and heir you are bearing there, my only child. All must go well!" He hung onto the ropes because the roll of the boat sent him stumbling, dressed in his usual coat of mail and armor.

"And who is to say it will be a boy!" Grace shouted back above the sound of the waves. "A girl would do well, a girl who loves the sea like me! Richard-in-Iron, I have birthed two other children on shipboard and I will do this one, too. Now stop your whimpering or I'll have you tossed overboard the minute it begins, and in that armor you will sink like a rock. I can't bear your petty fretting!"

"I ordered you to stay behind," her husband whined. "You have no business being out here in your condition.

There was no need for you to go to see Queen Elizabeth!"

"No need, indeed?" Grace O'Malley turned on him like an angry cow. "No need, and you going to the English court to be knighted. And for what? Was it not my own warriors who fought the rebels for the English crown in Connaught? The queen of England may knight you, but I will be there to get my share of due, I will!"

Richard sighed. What she said was true. Since their marriage, his exciting, impetuous wife had filled the de Burgh family castles and fortresses with men who stood by her loyally after the death of Donal O'Flaherty. There was something so strong, so wildly powerful in the tall, red-haired female leader, that the men obeyed her heartily. She it was who led the men to squelch a re-bellion of the Irish peasants for the sake of the de Burghs. Richard himself, a prince of the de Burgh clan in Connemara, yielded to her demand and married her with the stipulation that, after one year, either of them could divorce the other without question.

For days they had been at sea, Grace always on deck, ordering the sails and rudder, keeping in touch with the wind and tides, the salt spray pulling at her wild, titian hair. As they passed Waterford, she was standing at the bow. It was the place on the ship where she most loved to feel her power, the wind whipping her red hair into knots of curl. She felt a twinge of pain. The child was announcing its imminent exit from her womb. Richard, her elderly husband of eleven months, was in a state of nerves.

Now, with her child's birth becoming more and

more insistent, Grace left hold of the jib line and made her way to the tent-covered shelter on the deck.

The oarsmen were lounging at their poles while the sails carried the ship. They took note of Grace's careful steps into the tent and grinned and winked at one another. "We'll be having another passenger aboard soon here."

Grace was attended by the ship's surgeon, her husband frantically looking on. The boat pitched and rocked around Lands End and into St. George's Channel. It wasn't long before Richard de Burgh stepped out of the tent and raised his hands in the air, holding up a wet and squalling infant. "My son and heir!" he exulted.

A shout went up. Praises for their captain, the Queen of Pirates, Mistress of the Sea, Mother of Princes! Never mind the graying stud who chanced to have the privilege of fathering a child of Grace O'Malley!

Six days later, the oars were again put to use to battle the winds that never stopped and pull them up the Thames River to Londontown. They docked the galley ship and left only a few seamen aboard to guard the boat. The troop of Irish warriors strode boldly through the "civilized" streets of the city.

Londoners, young and old, hurried into the wooden shacks built heel to toe along the mud streets. They peered out through the cracked, old shutters at the huge, hairy Irish warriors, long hair chopped off just above their eyes, leather battle togs, barefoot, swinging battle axes at their sides.

Ahead of the troop walked Richard de Burgh, prince of the de Burghs of Connaught, and his consort, the beautiful Grace O'Malley O'Flaherty de Burgh. In her arms, Grace carried the tiny, sea-born infant wrapped in a voluminous shawl. Grace herself was gowned in a simple overdress of red muslin with embroidered designs following the cut of it low over her bosom, laced to her waist and flowing full below. Beneath it she wore a smock gathered at the throat, made of linen dyed her favorite color, royal saffron yellow. She had braided the forelock of her rich red hair into two parts and pulled them back together above a burst of red curls behind her head.

Richard, the fool of him, still wore his suit of chain metal armor along with the proper English-style puffed pantaloons and long snug stockings above his tall boots. Altogether, they made a strange procession through the streets of Londontown.

They were stopped at the gate to the queen's castle. A contingent of the queen's guard surrounded the wild-looking Irish warriors and led them through the grand halls of the huge building. Two dignified gentlemen approached Richard, and he produced the summons to prove he was to be honored by the queen. He and Grace were escorted with their entourage into the throne room where Elizabeth sat on the dais at the far end, waiting arrogantly.

Grace gazed around the room. She had never seen such elaborate appointments. Golden candelabra stood attached to the walls, heavy red velvet draperies swooped majestically at the tall, paned windows, the floor was thick with intricately designed carpets. The finest castles in Connaught were bare and primitive compared to this.

The room was busy with elaborately gowned ladies burdened with huge, heavy full skirts and the gentlemen wore velvet doublets and silken hose and high-heeled, buckled shoes. Everyone seemed to have a stiff, white ruff around his or her neck above the satins and silks and velvets of the costumes and a lot of jewelry. Compared to the effeminate appearance of the courtiers, Grace was proud of her stout soldiers in coarse, ankle-length trousers.

Grace caught the queen watching her being awed by the room and people and quickly the Irishwoman changed her attitude to one of pride and careless amusement. The queen of Connaught was not going to be subdued by the queen of England, and she let her know it with a haughty stare.

The most elaborate, large, crisply embroidered ruff was worn by the queen above a gown of dark blue velvet swathed with jewelry. The hair on her head was obviously a wig with stiff red curls set too far back on her head to be natural. Elizabeth sat on the dais three steps high at the end of the long room. The rich velvet of her huge skirts nearly enveloped her thin body and made her look small, but the lift of her chin, her bright, arrogant eyes, and the authoritative note in her voice when she spoke let them know she was in power.

The fine courtiers in the room looked disdainfully at the simple, country gown that Grace wore. She held her head up high, green eyes flashing, and stared boldly at their pretentious fashions and jewels. How would those fancy things hold up in a stormy gale in the Atlantic, she wondered with sarcasm.

The couple stood before the queen's throne. The

royal chamberlain announced them to her, and Richard went quickly down on one knee in a proper bow. Grace, holding her week-old infant in her arms, gave only a nod to Elizabeth and stood boldly gazing at Her Majesty.

A murmur went through the crowded courtiers in the hall at her audacity. The wild Irish warriors glared at the fancy folk, daring them to scorn their princess.

At first Elizabeth seemed surprised. Then she chose to ignore the clumsy, countrified Irishwoman and turned her attention to the Norman Irishman whom she had summoned to honor.

Placing the tip of a sword on his two shoulders, she announced, "Rise, Sir Richard de Burgh."

Suddenly, the tiny boy in his mother's arms screwed up his little red face and let out a squeaky squall. His tiny fists doubled and he squirmed in her grasp. The queen turned to Grace. "Would you like to have a wet nurse for that child while you are at court?" she asked, annoyed.

"That I will not." Grace was offended. "Sure, this child was born to me on the galley as we came across St. George's. No one cares for a child of my body but myself!"

With a quick movement, she yanked the strings of her smock and put the babe to her breast. He stopped squalling and nestled contentedly against her body.

All around the room, the ladies tittered in delighted shock and the regal gentlemen smirked. Immediately, Elizabeth sent a sharp look their way and the chatter quelled; the very noble group was stunned at her attitude toward the earthy, primitive woman.

"Was it difficult then to birth a babe on shipboard?"

"Not at all. I am an O'Malley. The O'Malleys have been the greatest mariners on the Atlantic for three hundred years. I was in the place where I belong, and my son was born to the sea like myself!"

"Ah, yes, and I understand that much of the army that Richard de Burgh led to battle in Connaught were troops you accumulated from your former husband, Donal O'Flaherty. I wish to show my appreciation to you for lending them to the cause of England. I will bestow upon you the honor of countess."

"I think not!"

Even Elizabeth was caught off guard and stared for a second, invisible eyebrows raised in offense. The people in the room caught their breaths. How dare this rough, barbaric woman refuse an honor from the queen? It could cost Grace O'Malley her head.

"You will not accept it?" Elizabeth angrily demanded an answer.

"I will not. Now then, how would it look for Grace O'Malley, the wife of a prince of the O'Flahertys and now the queen of the de Burghs, to come down to the role of a mere countess? You cannot give me peerage. We are equals, you and I. I will not!"

At first, Elizabeth's face grew red and her little brown eyes nearly started out of her face. Gradually, she regained her composure, staring intently at the tall, proud woman before her. Somehow, a look of respect came over the queen's pale face, along with slight amusement.

"Come up here to me, Grace O'Malley O'Flaherty de Burgh. Bring your child close to me."

What might this be? Grace wondered. Was the queen of England going to try to take her child from her? Perhaps she would like to foster him, as she had the young Hugh O'Neill, and try to make him an imitation of an Englishman. She would not! Grace would rip off that red wig and take off her head before she let the woman have her child! The sailors braced themselves, looking around at the crowd and daring anyone to harm their little prince.

However, the queen slowly stood up as Grace came close. While the congregation in the throne room stared, she gazed down at the tiny, hungry babe nestled to its mother's teat. Carefully she caressed the downy head with her fingertips. Then she spoke, royally, but sincere.

"I envy you, Grace O'Malley. It must be grand to sail the seas, to hunt the stag and boar in the wilds of Ireland, to bear a child on the high sea, to command your men on land and ship yourself instead of having to delegate underlings. The power, the hearty joy you must experience! How I would love to do as you do. Indeed, I do envy you."

A new murmur went up from the crowd, first of surprise and then, watching the queen curl the tiny hand of the babe around her finger, it quickly changed to overeager cooing.

"Well then, if you will not accept a boon from me, will you allow me to place an honor on your little prince?"

Richard de Burgh had been nervously watching the proceedings, first with shame at his wife's insolence, and then amazement at the queen's forbearance, and then great relief that Her Majesty was not going to toss Grace, child and all, into the Tower. He beamed, nodding his graying head. "How fine of you, Your Majesty. I am very proud of my firstborn, Theobald, my son and heir!"

Elizabeth reached out. "My sword."

When the blade was handed to her, she very carefully, with both hands, raised its tip and placed it on the tiny, round, bare shoulder of the infant.

"I dub thee Sir Theobald of the Ships."

* * *

"FOR FORTY YEARS GRACE O'MALLEY HAS BEEN THE NURSE OF ALL REBELLIONS IN CONNAUGHT!"

"THE WOMAN IS THE MOST NOTABLE TRAITRESS IN THE LAND."

"I HAVE A GALLOWS READY FOR THE PIRATE QUEEN AS SOON AS WE CAN FIND AND ARREST HER, ALTHOUGH HER MEN WILL FIGHT TO THE DEATH!"

So read the reports of Sir Richard Bingham, Lord Deputy of Elizabeth in the province of Connaught.

No sooner had Grace O'Malley arrived back in Ireland from her encounter with Queen Elizabeth than she put in motion her own plan of action. The year was up. Richard had thoughtlessly sworn to her that either of them could end their marriage without question if they chose. With her forces, Grace had gained control of every castle, townland, and village that the de Burghs possessed—and there were many. Her warriors were in place in each fortress ready to defend it for her sake against all other claimants. Queen of the O'Malley fleet of ships, queen of the fighting O'Flaherty clan, and princess of the de Burghs, Grace had what she wanted.

Standing on the top of the Carrickhooley tower house, she shouted down to her chagrined husband, "I divorce you!"

It was over.

Richard was stunned. True, he was not much of a fighter. He preferred peace and a tranquil married life beside his fire with his son on his lap. It was not to be. But he had thought that Grace would surely settle down after having borne his child and they would have a compatible existence.

Quietly he rode away without discussion and, finding a lovely spot near the coast of Clew Bay at Burrishoole, he built an abbey and retired to live there the last four years of his life.

But Grace O'Malley was far from retiring. She controlled the countryside. She owned three galley ships and two hundred seamen, besides her loyal troops on land. She lived in high style from "maintenance by land and sea." In other words, she took whatever she needed from the villages in exchange for protecting them from raiders and English dominance. She made the English ships pay a healthy toll for passing through "her" waters off Clew Bay, and she pirated Spanish merchants and French smugglers. Life was grand for her.

Her main base of operations was Clare Island. The castle there became a comfortable home, convenient to the open Atlantic. Her sons and daughter grew up, vibrant, lively people. She married her daughter to a near relative, Richard Burke, nicknamed "The Devil's Hook" by some of his English friends.

Sir Richard Bingham was made Lord Deputy by

Queen Elizabeth over Connaught, the west of Ireland. He got along well enough with Grace. When the Joyces and some Burke relatives rebelled against Bingham's rule, she assisted him to quell their efforts, verifying her loyalty to the lady who had knighted her son. As long as he was reasonable and did not make any effort to hinder her own arrangement, things went along nicely.

Then one day Grace got a message that tore her soul.

Sir Richard Bingham's brother John arrived in Connaught. It was he who stood to enforce Richard's edicts, collect tributes, and keep the people in tight control. "Captain" John Bingham loved his power and hated the Irish. With troops provided by the English, he set out to dominate the Celts of his brother's domain.

Owen, one of Grace's sons, had found that his simple castle and homestead in the countryside could be in jeopardy from all sides, the Joyces still kicking up rebellion and Captain John riding roughshod over the people, apparently making every attempt to keep down trouble. Owen O'Flaherty was still a loyal subject of the English crown, so he consulted Sir Richard on how he might avoid involvement in the upheavals. The Lord Deputy recommended that he move all his family and goods to an island not too far off the coast of Clew Bay. So he did. He removed all of his people, cattle, sheep, hogs, horses, donkeys, and family to just such a place and settled into a life of security and peace.

Then one night he heard a voice calling across the water.

"Ho, there! Captain John Bingham here! My peace-keeping soldiers are needing food and rest. Will you help us?"

"Owen O'Flaherty here!" Owen called back. "Is it the brother of my friend, Sir Richard Bingham? Sure, we will be glad to help you. Stay where you are. We'll come and bring you over."

A dozen boats set out from the island and soon the whole troop of the queen's soldiers were on the island being fed and comforted and secure for the night. But the O'Flaherty people were not so safe.

The eating and drinking went on deep into the night hours, ending with everyone merrily bedding down for a good rest. But Owen was waked when rough hands grabbed him and knotted ropes around his wrists and body. Eighteen of his own warriors were also caught off guard by their "guests" and thoroughly hog-tied to one another. They were thrown into the darkness of the keep while Captain John and his troop ransacked Owen's home and tormented his household.

With boats and ropes, John Bingham herded four hundred head of cattle off the island, followed by nearly fifty brood mares and stud horses and some three hundred sheep, every worthy animal that belonged to the son of Grace O'Malley. The family and servants were left alone on the island with no food, warm clothes, or comforts.

The horse soldiers of John Bingham dragged the trussed up Owen O'Flaherty and his men nearly thirty miles on foot across the rocky hills from Clew Bay to Ballynahinch, herding the livestock along with them. There Captain John decided to set up camp and settle matters.

Beside the campfires that evening, his troops were

entertained by the hangings of each of the eighteen workmen from the O'Flaherty castle, while they drank and fought over Owen's property. Even Theobald O'Toole, a ninety-year-old man who had served Owen O'Flaherty since he was a child, was strung up to choke to death in the light of the fires.

Owen himself was tossed into a corner of an officer's tent, still bound tightly. He lay there all that night listening to the cries for mercy of his friends as they were hung one by one. He heard the shouts of the English soldiers, laughing as the victims kicked and struggled at the end of the noose.

There he lay all the next day, wondering what was to become of him, what delights John Bingham had planned for amusement when it was Owen's turn to die. It was midnight the next night when a hue and cry went up in the camp. The soldiers were being attacked! Immediately, someone ran into the tent and stabbed Grace's oldest son twelve times.

Mistake. There was no attack. Oh, well, that was the end of Owen O'Flaherty. Captain John Bingham packed up his troops and herded the livestock off to the lands of his brother, Sir Richard, while he took his troops out to raid, murder, and rob every homestead in Connaught. He took thousands of cattle and sheep from the peasants, burned their fields and homes, and left them to starve. It was a time of horror in Ireland.

Grace was clever in battle, but her army measuring in the hundreds was no competition for the thousands of the queen's troops under John Bingham. She complained to the Lord Deputy, Sir Richard Bingham.

"How can this be, that your brother killed my son

and ravaged his home and family? Have I not supported you and the queen with my men and supplies? Am I and my territory next on his plan to completely destroy Connaught?"

Richard was sympathetic. "I cannot account for my brother's methods of maintaining government authority over the undisciplined peasants in Ireland. My condolences on the loss of your son. Surely I will speak to him about this. And I will give you letters of protection, which will prevent any further distress to your family. However, I urge you to leave the territory at Carrickhooley and move yourself and your attendants to my headquarters twelve miles east of there that no further errors are made."

She did. Gathering together her herd of a thousand cattle and her warriors and herdsmen, she left the safety of her castles and began the move.

They had not traveled five miles inland, away from her ships and warriors, before a troop of English soldiers came down on them. They were killed and scattered and all the livestock rounded up and run off. Grace herself, a strong but middle-aged woman, with her hands tied behind her back, was shoved and forced to walk over the stony hills. The leader of the band was Captain John Bingham.

At last they came to Captain John's destination, Sir Richard's headquarters. As she stumbled through the stone gates of the fortress, Grace saw workmen high on a scaffold. They were building a gallows, "a new gallows for her final days," ordered by Sir Richard Bingham.

"So it comes to this," Grace O'Malley thought. "I have been lied to, betrayed, robbed, brutalized, and now I will die, and all at the hands of the English. It is going on all over Ireland, the deputies of the queen raping the land and starving the people. But is Elizabeth aware of this? Does she know that even her friends among the Irish, people like me who trusted and supported her, are being treated thus? Would she do anything about it?"

Sir Richard prepared letters to the queen, letters describing the traitorous acts of Grace O'Malley O'Flaherty de Burgh, for forty years a thorn in the side of those of Queen Elizabeth's duly sworn representatives who were trying to bring order to the province of Connaught. The letters were sent by messenger across Ireland and from Dublin port to Holyhead to London. The queen would recognize what devoted subjects she had in the Bingham brothers, working so hard in her service.

Grace lay in darkness on the dank stone floor of the castle keep. Her men who fought for her so loyally were scattered or dead. All of her power was lost. Her arms ached from the flesh-cutting ropes that still held her hands behind her. But she was not afraid of the gallows. She was furious!

She squirmed herself upright against the slimy, wet stone wall. The ever present spiders of Ireland walked across her face and skin. She struggled with the ropes on her wrists and ankles. Drawing her knees up close to her chest she waited, ready with her boots to immasculate the first man who came to drag her to the gallows.

A sound of metal on metal, then the clink of swords, and men's voices echoed in the small, black space.

"Come!" she shouted. "Come and find what Grace

O'Malley has for you, you son of a dog!"

"Son of a dog, am I?" came an amused voice. "So then, did you marry off your daughter to a dog, Grace O'Malley?"

"You, the Devil's Hook! How came you here?"

"Not all of your men were murdered, Grace," Richard Burke said. "One of them found his way to Corraun to tell my wife that her mother was going to be hung. Perhaps he thought she would want to be here for the occasion."

Grace felt him reach for her in the dark. "Here you, guard," he called. "Light a torch so that I don't break my neck. And set yourself to taking off her bonds. They must be most uncomfortable after three days in this hole."

The ropes came off. Richard lifted her to her feet, but she could not stand. He demanded another guard to come and help the lady out of the dungeon.

While the guard was gone he said, "We have heard all about it, Lady de Burgh. The betrayal and slaughter of my wife's brother, Owen. The attack on you and your men after being lured into the country away from your seamen and fortresses by Richard Bingham. I begged permission to take you out of here on my pledge that you will never rebel against them again. They know I have friends in Dublin so they agreed, rather reluctantly, I'm certain. And, sure, we know how the Binghams have raped the poor farmers of Connaught, stealing all their animals and destroying their crops. I believe John Bingham is truly set to destroy all the Irish by way of famine. And I'm not knowing any way to stop them."

Shaking on her trembling legs, rubbing her blood-less arms, Grace spoke with ominous quiet. "I know a way."

The work on the fine new gallows came to a halt. Young Richard Burke placed his mother-in-law in a wagon and, riding beside her with a contingent of guards, they left the castle yard.

The Bingham brothers, Sir Richard and Captain John, stood at a window in the castle wall, watching her leave and seething with fury. The Pirate Queen who had literally ruled all the area around Clew Bay and the islands and the lands of Connaught was slipping out of their hands. She was the only one with enough power to give them trouble, and they thought they had her! Richard's letters about her to Queen Elizabeth had re-ceived no response, thereby giving them silent assent to any way they chose to take care of the problem.

They didn't dare to refuse the Devil's Hook, so named by his English cronies in Dublin who couldn't translate his Irish title. With his friends in high places, they might offend the wrong person and be relieved of their command.

Grace arrived at Kildavnet, the castle she had given to Richard Burke and her daughter as a wedding gift. Actually, her principle reason for the gift was to secure the entrance to Clew Bay with allies at Achill Island, only five miles from her base at Clare Island. No one could enter Clew Bay without being spotted and de-terred by her seamen.

"Grace O'Malley, I promised, I am bound by my word, that you will never make war with the Binghams." Richard told her sternly as he settled her in his castle.

"Now rest yourself, Lady de Burgh. Remember, you are not getting any younger."

His words bristled in the core of Grace O'Malley. The tall, sturdily built woman in her fifties was far from a frail, old woman. Grand sea air, good food, the brisk exercise of sailing ships and managing cattle had kept her cheeks red and her eyes bright and her physical strength powerful.

"Do not make war on the Binghams," Richard said.

"Nor will I," she granted.

The next morning a strange sight could be seen if a person could stand off the shore beside the castle, which was unlikely. A purple robe with yellow lining whipped in the sea winds, hanging from the highest south window, showing now the purple side, then the saffron. The cloak had been a trademark of Grace O'Malley for many years. Faded it was and shabby around the edges, but it was her favorite and recognized as her own.

Five miles away, a grizzled sailor stood on the deck of a galley ship moored to Clare Island. Marty MacDuffy grinned behind his bush of gray whiskers as he held a spyglass to his eye.

"The messenger said she was near to hanged," he said to himself. "The messenger said she was whipped, helpless, all beaten down, that her life was over. I knew better." He raised his voice to a shout. "You there, boy! Call the men! Get to your stations! Our captain calls!"

From the high window at Kildavnet, Grace watched a ship silently glide away from Clare and put to water, slowly coming toward Achill. She smiled.

By the time her banner ship reached the docking

site near Kildavnet, she was waiting for it. Without bothering to say farewell to her daughter and son-in-law, Grace O'Malley, the Pirate Queen, was in control of her life once more.

Setting her sails to the South, the ship rounded the southern coast of Ireland toward St. George's Channel.

They docked at Greenwich, England, where Queen Elizabeth was holding court. It was not so easy to gain admission to the palace. Elizabeth was also getting older and more cautious. Grace was delayed, examined, and required to answer a written questionnaire with eighteen queries. The queen chose to receive her in the privacy of her library instead of before a covy of twittering courtiers. At last Grace stood once more before the queen of England.

As before, Grace did not kowtow to the woman she considered her equal. Elizabeth sized her up. While Elizabeth had spent the past forty years in comfortable palaces, Grace O'Malley O'Flaherty de Burgh had been riding the open sea. Her hair was streaked with gray compared to Elizabeth's perennial red wig. Her complexion was ruddy. Grace still stood taller than England's queen, straight and proud. She wore a leathern doublet over a loose, white, man's shirt, and her skirts were heavy wool above her boots.

Elizabeth seemed to be smaller than ever, swallowed up in her huge skirts and heavy jewels. She also was showing her age, even though her face was powdered to death white and her eyebrows were shaved off, a fashionable attempt for a look of youthful innocence.

Did Elizabeth need to fear this wild-looking woman? She thought not. Grace O'Malley was not afraid of her.

There would be no need for Grace to lie.

"I'm hearing evil reports of you, O'Malley," Elizabeth scolded. "Rebellion. Insurrection. Traitorousness."

"I have no need to play traitor to you," Grace replied boldly. "You know where I have stood these many years. I and my men have fought for your cause in Connaught and on the sea. It is your own men who lie to you. Your Lord Deputy, Richard Bingham, and his murdering brother, John Bingham."

Grace told the queen about the raids on the people of Connaught, the starvation, the killing. It appeared that Elizabeth was not impressed. Ireland had been a thorn in her side for forty years, getting even more rebellious in the last fifteen years. If her deputies felt they must take drastic measures to conquer that Irish defiance against their proper rulers, then she would not chastise them for one province.

Neither did the story of Sir Richard's deception in order to arrest Grace trouble the queen. Heaven knew she had done her share of trickery and sometimes even a gift of tainted wine when it was necessary to eliminate troublesome opposition.

Then the Pirate Queen told Elizabeth in detail about the sneak attack on Grace's son, his trust of the English, his support of the Crown, and his friendly offer of hospitality that was rewarded with his own murder.

"Your son?" Elizabeth frowned. "Which son?"

Grace knew that her oldest son's name would carry little influence with the queen of England. Somehow, she must dent the hard shell of power that had grown to armor during the forty years reign. Lie to her? She would not stoop to that.

"If I told you it was Theobald of the Ships, the tiny babe you knighted more than thirty years ago, would that move you to stop the carnage in Connaught?" Grace asked. "I doubt it. But do you realize that, even as I stand here pleading for my livelihood and the salvation of my territories, that young man is leading his men to fight for England and the queen? He remains loyal to you even though his brother was murdered and his brother's family impoverished by your representatives."

Silence. For a long time Elizabeth studied the flames in the nearby fireplace, her small, brown eyes staring at the flickering light.

Grace said nothing. She had done what she could. If Elizabeth did not appreciate honesty, then it was beyond Grace to beg. She waited, watching those same flames consuming a log the way England was determined to consume Ireland.

At last Queen Elizabeth spoke. "I remember a little lad presented to me in court, a tiny, helpless babe who caught my barren heart by its strings. I believe I saw in that bit of humanity greatness and integrity. It seems I did not err. Go home to Ireland, Grace O'Malley. Live out your years in peace as I can never live mine."

Before Grace's journey home was complete, couriers from the queen of England carried parchment orders swiftly across the water and by horse to the province of Connaught in Ireland. Summoned to the queen's court, Richard and John Bingham scurried to obey, sure that some fine rewards waited them for their grand efforts to control England's territories. Upon their arrival in London, they were promptly sent to the Tower.

In a proper amount of time, they were both relieved of their heads.

∽◉∾

Both Grace O'Malley and Queen Elizabeth died in 1603.
Two queens, rulers in parallel years over their domains. Grace
was buried in the abbey she built on Clare Island and lives on
still in awestruck legends among the people of Connaught.

Mabel Bagenal, the Elopement

Queen Elizabeth had a clever means of con-
trolling the Irish leaders (besides an occa-
sional gift of poisoned wine). She would "in-
vite" them to visit her at the palace in London
and then insist that they remain as "the guest
of the queen," where she could keep an eye on
them. So it was with young Hugh O'Neill.

The boy, descendant next in line of the
O'Neill kings, was fostered by Sir Henry
Sidney and his family. He became a favorite
of the queen, handsome, fabulously dressed,
bright and popular. And he watched.

rs. Barnwell, who is that stunning man talking to
brother Henry by the door?"

"Don't be impertinent, Mabel Bagenal, calling your
own sister by her married name. You want to remind
me that I had to marry a man old enough to be my
grandfather in order to marry at all. There are almost

no eligible worthy Englishmen in Ireland, and well you know it. Our brother Henry compelled me to marry Sir Patrick and rid himself of one sister. That man you ask about. Forget about him. That is Hugh O'Neill, an Irishman, and utterly forbidden to you."

Mabel and Evleen watched the two men standing across the room by the wide open, tall, oak doors of the Bagenal mansion. Outside the entrance, the summer sun shone brilliantly on the green lawn, where guests could be seen entertaining themselves at croquet and pall-mall. Inside the large entry hall, the velvet draperies were drawn aside, allowing the sunlight to reflect on the gleaming flagstone floor. More guests milled around the grand room gossiping, flirting, and laughing, lords and ladies, prosperous settlers, landlords, from nearby plantations, the elite of Ireland's Ascendancy class. The women wore pale-colored, summer gowns even though their bouffant skirts weighed heavily and swayed with every step. Gentleman also were dressed in lighter weight doublets and buckled shoes instead of riding boots. From an invisible gallery behind the portiers came the strains of lively music. It was to be a grand affair of games and music and sumptuous cuisine, introducing the community to Henry Bagenal's masterpiece of a new house.

"An Irishman, is it?" Mabel continued to question. "Indeed, Evleen, he is dressed like an English lord. His cloak and doublet are fine quality. And his manners, look how arrogantly he stands, how he holds his cup and salutes Henry as they talk, the lift of his chin. No Irish barbarian that!"

"Henry hates him, as he hates all Irishmen, but he is

afraid to rebuff him or turn him from the door. O'Neill was fostered by Sir Henry Sidney, the Lord Deputy, and his family in England. Even Queen Elizabeth was charmed by him as he grew up in her court. Now he has come back to Ireland to claim his rights as the earl of Tyrone."

"An earl then? Well now, I believe I must meet this intriguing man."

Evleen Barnwell looked sharply at her beautiful sister with an immediate refusal on her lips. The married sister was dressed quite simply in dark blue silk, but Mabel was gowned in brilliant blue satin cut low over her bosom to enhance her slim waist above the full skirt. A charming little, white ruff surrounded her throat, but her jewelry was light and she wore her golden hair in a halo of rich, shining braids to hold it in place for the day-long soiree.

This Hugh O'Neill had not been invited of course. Not an Irishman in the land was welcome at Bagenal's estate, unless they were servants. It was quite obvious that O'Neill knew that and came anyway. Henry had to use the transparent excuse of ignorance that the earl of Tyrone had only recently come to Ireland from London and his invitation was overlooked.

Mabel was much sought after at nineteen years old but, as Evleen stated, there were few qualified Englishmen among the planters in Ireland who were single, wealthy, and of pure Anglo-Saxon stock fit to marry the sister of Henry Bagenal, marshall of Ireland. And brother Henry was taking great care to see that, when she married, it would make a contact for himself in the London palace of the queen. But Mabel was also determined that she would not marry just to suit her brother's preference. She would choose the man for her.

Suddenly Evleen smiled, a merry, impish smile. "Mabel, my dear, I think it would be delightfully amusing to watch Henry squirm if you flirt with Hugh O'Neill. Come, I will see to it that you have the opportunity."

Evleen searched the grand rooms of the Bagenal house there in Newry, and finally found her ageing husband, Sir Patrick Barnwell, in a cluster of older men before the fire in the magnificently wainscoted drawing room. Pulling him aside, she whispered to him. He did not look pleased, but he grudgingly made his apologies to his cronies and left with her.

In minutes, the white-haired gentleman was escorting the two sisters across the gleaming flags of the huge entry hall to the place where Henry Bagenal, the marshal of all the queen's forces in Ireland, stood tolerating the company of the Irish earl. William Warren had joined them, a fellow settler who carefully knew no enemies because he was designing himself a prosperous future among the plantations in the Pale. His position as landowner gave him access to the company of the Ascendancy, but he made a good friend of Hugh O'Neill, too, to be sure he was not counted as an enemy to the Irish chieftains either.

Henry turned red with repressed anger when his sisters appeared at his side, Sir Patrick with them, but could do no less than introduce his sisters and brother-in-law to Hugh O'Neill, all the while glaring at Evleen for her obvious manipulations to bedevil him.

The earl was not overly tall, but there was a confidence about him that gave him stature. His dark brown beard was neatly trimmed and his brown eyes had a light in them, a light of pleasure or perhaps ambition, or was it spite? It was hard to discern, but it served to make Mabel curious. Sturdily built, he was, and muscular. His crisp, white ruff accented his powerful frame under his elaborately embroidered black velvet doublet and short cloak.

As he bowed his head over Mabel's slim, white hand, his eyes sparked with amusement. She was a beauty and he could see quite well that his courtly attention to Henry's lovely sister was rankling the man so that he could barely speak the proper words of introduction.

A few polite phrases of welcome and Evleen, smiling wickedly at her brother, drew her husband away and took Barnwell once more to his elderly companions in the drawing room.

After a few proper banal amenities Henry stuttered, "Mabel, my dear, I believe our friends are waiting for you at the pall-mall courts out on the lawn. You must not keep our guests waiting to enjoy a game."

"Indeed, I should not. Thank you, brother, for reminding me of my hostess duties." Then, smiling a bit too sweetly at Hugh O'Neill, Mabel asked, "Would you care to escort me to the courts, Sir?"

The handsome Irishman was clearly well aware of the game the sisters were playing, teasing their pompous, arrogant brother, and he joined in enthusiastically, delighted at the chance to annoy the Englishman. Bagenal's reputation for his treatment of the despised Irish was common knowledge in the queen's court. "I am honored, lovely lady. It will be a pleasure," he said and swept the pretty, golden-haired maiden out through the wide door onto the sunlit lawns.

Bagenal fairly steamed. It was not a game to him. He hated the Irish and wished no part of them, except what he could take from them. If he was to be stuck in these hinterlands due to his father's unfortunate prowess with dueling pistols, he would make a stunning success of it. Someday he would have the largest plantation on the island, and if Irish heads must roll and Irish blood saturate the earth, by the heavens, he would do it! Some had already met that fate as his lands expanded.

Now this insolent Irish earl, a pet of the queen while he grew up in the royal court in London, because of his foster father being the Lord Deputy, was flirting with Henry's beautiful sister! Whether or not the women had plotted this introduction as a jest, Henry would put an immediate stop to it somehow.

Mabel had a grand time that day, courteously escorted through the games and musicals and partaking of delicious sweetmeats in the house and grounds of Henry Bagenal's mansion.

However, brother Henry seemed to be at every turn, reminding Mabel that she must see to the guests' luncheon, pointing out a special lady who needed proper attention from her hostess, urging O'Neill away to meet certain important nobles. Each of his clumsy attempts to separate the two failed. Somehow they casually went off to attend to all those things together! Henry Bagenal's dark hazel eyes scowled at Hugh O'Neill's fatuous attentions to his single sister.

O'Neill was enjoying Henry Bagenal's vexation. Besides having the delight of a beautiful girl's company, Hugh had other reasons to take pleasure in agitating the marshall. He had learned upon coming home to Ireland that more than once Bagenal had used his position as marshall of the law and military in Ireland to steal, lie, and kill in order to get anything he wanted. Irish people had suffered outrages at his hands. No more. Hugh O'Neill was in the country now, calling together his fellow Irish kings and lords. He himself had sat upon the Lia Fail stone and secretly been crowned *The O'Neill*, descendant of the grand line of O'Neill high kings. He was determined that soon Ireland would belong to the Irish again.

At dusk, as the festivities wound down, with William Warren waiting with horses for their ride to O'Neill's home at Dungannon, the 39-year-old earl of Tyrone stood in the darkening garden of the house and gazed down at the beautiful girl. He took her hand.

"Lovely Mabel, I thank you for obliging me with your company this day. I have not had such cheerful female company since the passing of my wife, the sister of Red Hugh O'Donnell. In your confidence I must admit that, although your beauty is breathtaking, my principal reason for taking possession of you was to aggravate your brother Henry. I know he has a grand dislike for me, an Irishman, coming boldly into his home. I could not pass up the opportunity to watch his agitation as I escorted his prized sister. But now, having spent many hours with you, I have a greater reason to seek you out. Mabel Bagenal, you are sweet natured, pleasant, good humored. I have thoroughly enjoyed your company this day. In spite of my confession and in spite of your brother's disapproval, may I have your permission to come here to Newry to see you on occasion?"

Mabel was surprised, but not for long. It was so exciting! In one short afternoon, she had found Hugh O'Neill to be thoughtful, gallant, and a clever playmate. And, to think that the earl of Tyrone, lately from the queen's court in London, found her enticing! He was a brave warrior, appointed a leader of the queen's armies in Ireland. Why then would she not want him to call? If Henry wasn't pleased, let him stew about it.

"My lord, I would be pleased to become better acquainted with you," she murmured demurely, but her blue eyes were shining with pleasure.

"I am honored." The earl of Tyrone kissed her hand and bowed low. Then he ran off across the darkening lawns to meet his waiting friend. Mabel laughed when she saw him leap joyfully across a bed of flowers before he disappeared behind the shrubs.

And so it began. At every occasion, invited or not, Hugh O'Neill appeared at the grand house. Whenever possible, he and Mabel would disappear into the garden or the drawing room or even the stables. Henry stewed and simmered and often came to a boil, taking his sister aside and berating her for her attentions to this rebel, this barbarian, this *Irishman!* He dared not confront O'Neill. Hugh was still a pet of Queen Elizabeth and apparently in her service in Ireland. Henry might find his head on a pike, as did Hugh's great uncle, Shane O'Neill, if he offended the earl. But Henry furiously fought his sister.

It was a lovely time that summer. In spite of Henry's

frustration, he dared not turn down too often the couple's rendezvous. They went riding together over the meadows and into shady green glens. They picnicked on top of the Mourne Mountains where they could see King John's castle and the Irish Sea. They strolled the gardens around the Bagenal house and laughed when they became lost in the shrubs of the maze. Oh, it was a good time.

In the late summer, Hugh O'Neill appeared at the Bagenal house on an important errand. Escorted into the drawing room, he stood before the marshall of all Ireland.

"Sir," he said confidently and without hesitation. "I'm sure you know that I have found your lovely sister irresistible. I care greatly about her. I have good reason to believe she cares for me, also. Marshall Henry Bagenal, may I ask your beautiful sister, Mabel, to marry me?"

Henry sputtered and stumbled, trying desperately to come up with an acceptable reason to deny the request, a reason that would not offend O'Neill but would put a stop to this infuriating courtship.

At last he stuttered, "I'm afraid that is not possible, Your Lordship. You see, um, my sister, um, is of a delicate nature. Your estate at Dungannon lies in the hinterlands, far away from civilization. I fear for her health and her life surrounded by feudal chieftains and their wild, barbaric ways. No, my lord, I apologize, but I'm sure, if you care for her, you would not want to subject her to such dangers."

Hugh O'Neill was ready for him. "I am in the process of building the finest home in the province of

Ulster. She shall have servants and guards and strong stone walls to protect her. And there is not an Irish chieftain in all of Ulster who would dare to offend the bride of The O'Neill. Nor would they want to, for they have great respect for me."

Henry grew more confident as O'Neill begged for his sister's hand. He framed his refusal more sternly then.

"My apologies, Lord Hugh, but I feel that, for my sister's good, she should not marry into the Irish. She is accustomed to enjoyable occupations and visitors and refinements. I know she would be very unhappy there. And it is not safe. I beg your pardon, Lord Hugh, but I cannot endorse your courtship."

Hugh stood tall and his dark brown eyes shot fire. "Could it be, Henry Bagenal, that it is not affection for your sister that affords your decision, but guilt? Guilt, knowing that you have built your home on the land of Manus McMahon, whom you *murdered*?"

Bagenal went white with rage. He stood up. "McMahon was not murdered. He was legally tried and found guilty of sedition!"

"His home was invaded by you after he was promised peace, and he was arrested, tried before a court of rag-tag soldiers, and hanged, all within twenty-four hours!" O'Neill's voice was low and tight. "Now this very house stands on his lands you stole, forfeited with his own blood. I am not such a fool that I cannot see your designs!"

His face almost purple with rage, Bagenal went to the door and called footmen. "Lord Hugh O'Neill will be leaving now," he ordered. "He will be escorted from the grounds of this house and will not be welcome to enter again!"

Hugh scooped up his plumed hat and walked firmly to the door. He turned and spoke. "For the sake of my love for your sister, I will do you no personal harm. But, Henry Bagenal, beware!"

No sooner had Hugh's horse left the grounds than Henry called his sister to him.

"Mabel, call your ladies and pack your things. You are going to take a holiday, a *long* holiday, to your sister Evleen's home in Turvey!"

"Turvey! That is fifty-five miles from here!"

"That is right. And eighty miles from Dungannon. You are never to see that barbarian, Hugh O'Neill, again. And certainly you will not entertain any thoughts of marriage to him. You will *never* receive my permission to do such an outrageous thing. Do you hear?"

Mabel's blue eyes narrowed to glittering slits. Her cheeks went red as fire. Her voice was quiet and cold.

"I hear." So she heard, and his petty jealousy of the Irishman, his self-centered decision to thwart her happiness, his bigotry toward all of the people of the island sent her into a seething fury. Somehow, she must contact Hugh O'Neill. Somehow, over the miles, they would find each other again and fulfill their love. She packed her bags and was firmly escorted by six horsemen southward over the country to Turvey, just in case she had any ideas of running to Dungannon or sending a message to O'Neill to intercept her journey.

At the door of the large, stone house of Sir Patrick Barnwell, Mabel gave her sister a tearful salutation. "Evleen, Henry sends me to you to get me as far away from Hugh O'Neill as he can. I love Hugh. He wants to marry me. Henry says no. Oh, Evleen, I can't bear it!"

Evleen Barnwell welcomed her sister gladly. "It's going to be grand having you here. Don't you worry about it. We will take care of it. Now then, the company of my ancient husband drags daily. We will have a ball and many entertainments and festivities in your honor. Old Barnwell does not enjoy music and games, but he cannot deny me the pleasure of having frolics for my sister. Indeed, we are a long way from Ulster, but not far enough, my sister. Not far enough!"

True to Evleen's plans, Turvey came to life with music and colorful people and frolicsome activities. And Hugh O'Neill.

He was there at every function. When Mabel chose to slip away with him into the garden, Evleen kept the guests too busy to take note. The girl glowed with secret joy, and Hugh O'Neill's attentions to her were tender, caring.

After O'Neill's very first visit to the Barnwell mansion, Mabel appeared wearing a magnificent golden chain around her collar. She explained it to Evleen as "a betrothal gift."

Evleen was ecstatic. "Henry Bagenal will not marry you off to a relic, my girl. We must lay our plans. I must talk secretly to Hugh O'Neill."

The innocent parties continued. Evleen invited many of the finest gentlefolk in the English settlement around Dublin and inside the Pale. The Barnwell mansion was often alive with music and happy chatter. Sir Patrick became weary and irritated and demanded of his sprightly wife when she would end it, when her sister would leave so that he could have peace and quiet again.

"Soon, my husband," Evleen answered, a feisty sparkle in her eyes. "Very soon now."

On the first day of August, the festival of Lughnasa, Evleen hosted an especially elaborate event. Hugh O'Neill entertained her guests with his usual energetic personality and clever wit.

The activities waned late, but the guests sat entranced around the drawing room fireplace, listening to his merry conversation. No one noticed in the twilight that one important person was no longer among them.

Mabel Bagenal had disappeared up the stairs early in the evening. She donned a red velvet cloak over her party gown and gathered together some things out of her boudoir into a small bag. Silently she made her way down the back stairs that led to the stables and slipped through the garden hedges. Then she ran swiftly in her pretty satin slippers across the wide lawn toward a grove of trees.

In the evening shadows, a very nervous William Warren sat astride a big horse that was pillioned with a thick pad behind the saddle. When the girl came up to him, Warren jumped down and helped her to get firmly comfortable on the pillion. As soon as she was securely settled and holding tight, he remounted and turned the horse westward toward Drumcondra Castle, his home.

"For the sake of heaven, hold on tight!" he ordered. "What I am about to do can cost me my head if it doesn't come off just right. As it is, if your brother finds out I am part of this, my fate in Ireland is doomed. Do not fall or get injured in any way! We must ride like the

wind in order to get to Drumcondra and be ready in time."

"In time." The words rang like a song in Mabel's heart. *In time* for the most wonderful event of her life.

The pair galloped hard in the deepening dusk and on into the night. Warren urged the powerful horse frantically, so nervous that he had put himself in danger of alienating the marshal. He could not imagine why he had agreed to this, except that Hugh O'Neill was also one of those whose influence he cultivated. The whole scheme was outrageous, and he was doing it for the favor of a rascal Irishman.

As for Mabel, she was exhilarated, riding through the night, her hair whipping in the wind. She was gloriously happy and not the least fearful of her brother's reaction when he learned what had happened.

They arrived at the Warren castle. Mabel was helped by a housemaid to a beautifully appointed bedchamber, where she refreshed her appearance after the jarring ride. Then she sat on a wide windowsill and waited.

Before long, another horse's hooves could be heard clopping onto the cobblestones of the gateyard. From the top of the stairs, Mabel saw Warren welcome an elderly gentleman in cleric clothing, the very Protestant bishop of Meath, Thomas Jones.

"Is the bridal party here yet?" the bishop asked William Warren.

"The bride is here, but the rest are not."

"I hope they hurry," Jones said nervously. "I want to be done with this business and gone from here before Henry Bagenal hears of it."

"You are in no more hurry than I," Warren said.

"But if you are worried, why did you offer to officiate?"

"And why not," Jones answered bluntly. "Why did you agree to confiscate the beautiful maiden for Hugh O'Neill? It is because he is a fine man, a blessing to his kinsmen here in Ireland, and a favorite of the queen. I cannot condone the evil things Henry Bagenal has done to the Irish, he and all those greedy ones like him. The evicting, the raids, the illegal shenanigans, the killing of the Irish lords whose families owned this land for centuries. And the Irish equipped neither with the knowledge of warfare nor the tools of modern conflict to resist them. If the fair Mabel has learned to love Hugh O'Neill and it is her honest, uncoerced wish to marry him properly in the sight of God, then why may I not assist her?"

"I see," Warren said, rubbing his hands in agitation. "But I wish he would hurry before others find her gone and come searching. I need O'Neill here in case I have to be defended."

"No one will notice until breakfast," Bishop Jones assured him. "That clever sister of hers will see to that."

At the words of the bishop, a sort of wonderful peace settled over Mabel's joyful spirit. Indeed, Hugh O'Neill was attractive, gallant, and exciting, but it was true that he was also a hero in the eyes of his people. He was a man raised with all of the benefits of an English aristocrat and a soldier well trained in English warfare, who came back to Ireland to be among his own, a champion and a model for them. What was it that the Sidney family called him when he left them in London? A fox, an Irish fox, determined to return to its inherent wild ways when it rejoined its own kind.

Dawn was just breaking when a clatter of many hooves sounded outside. At a window, Mabel saw several riders, eleven altogether, dismounting their steeds and entering the high, oaken doors of the castle. Hugh was there.

With her heart pounding, she waited until her name was called from downstairs.

Slowly she descended the wide staircase. On her head was a crown of flowers, and a soft, wispy veil drifted down over her hair and shoulders. She was gowned in shimmering blue and white silk, which trailed behind her on the steps. The golden chain of love lay around her shoulders and on her breast.

At the foot of the stairs, the earl of Tyrone gazed up at his beautiful bride with rapt adoration such as Mabel had not before seen in his eyes. That look, that overwhelming love, was worth all the danger, fury, and ugliness that would be forthcoming from her selfish, bigoted brother.

Behind Hugh, ten young men clustered, swords sheathed at their sides, delighted to be part of the escapade and stand witness to the wedding of Hugh O'Neill and the sister of Henry Bagenal. Also, the young men would be on hand should anything go wrong.

As Hugh took the hand of lovely Mabel, his eyes never left hers and he whispered, "You are majestic. Someday you will be a queen as you were made to be."

Mabel had no idea what he meant by that promise, but it mattered not. She walked as on a cloud on his arm through the great hall of the mansion house and into the drawing room, where the bishop waited at the hearthside.

Lord Hugh O'Neill and Mabel Bagenal stood side by side before the minister, stated their vows solemnly and joyfully, and were eternally joined together.

On the final "amen," the group shouted blessings on the pair, and Bishop Jones gathered his sacraments together quickly and made ready to depart.

"Will you not stay long enough to share the toast to the bride and groom?" William Warren asked.

"I will not. I shall toast their happiness when I am by myself in front of my own safe fireplace as soon as I get there!"

"Well then, come, my friends," William Warren said. "The festive board awaits. Food and drink for all. We will toast the bride and groom!"

The celebration at Drumcondra lasted five days. Certainly, Mabel became weary of the party and wanted to go on to Dungannon with her husband, but he told her "no." Surely Henry had heard of her disappearance by now. Would he not be scouring all of Ireland for her, and wouldn't Dungannon be the first place he would search?

Anyway, her grand stone house was not quite finished. However, at least their connubial quarters in the mansion were being completed and prepared with fine furnishings and draperies and expensive appointments from London. He wanted those apartments ready when he took her to her new home.

It was true. When they rode into the courtyard of the grand mansion at Dungannon, Henry Bagenal had already been there, red in the face, bellowing fury and challenging anyone who claimed his sister had willingly married Hugh O'Neill, the barbarian. No doubt, if he had caught them in the wilderness or on the highway, Hugh would have been murdered and Henry would have taken Mabel home as if rescued from an abductor.

"We must make it clear to my dear brother-in-law that we are married and will remain so," Hugh said jovially. "My lovely little bride, don't you think it would be appropriate if I sent word to him to send your dowry along right away? How much do you think I should ask? It should be enough to impress him of your value."

"And enough to send him into seizures," she amended with a delighted grin.

The earl of Tyrone burst into laughter. "Agreed! How about one thousand pounds in silver? Will that do it?"

"I should think so."

In the months that followed, Mabel understood what the bishop meant when he spoke about Hugh O'Neill's subversive activities. Hugh was secretly gathering the Irish chieftains together. They had crowned him The O'Neill, as close as the Irish came to naming him high king.

As time went on, Hugh's cousin, Red Hugh O'Donnell, the earl of Tirconnell, joined forces with Hugh, and they led the chieftains in harassing the English. O'Neill was skilled in the ways of English warfare from his years of learning and training in England. He used their own tactics against them. He was one step in front of them everywhere. Like pestering gadflies, they struck the English here and there, ambushments, surprise attacks, skirmishes with mercenary gallowglass soldiers. He also fought with guerrilla maneuvers, popping out of the thick forests and caves at the most inconvenient times to catch the English troops off guard. Sometimes there were major battles which the Irish did not always win, but they did not lose either.

Hugh O'Neill soon became the hero of the Irish people, their prince, their leader and hope for freedom. The cousins were determined that someday they would drive the English soldiers out of their land and reclaim the rights of the Irish people to govern themselves according to the democratic Brehon laws, as they had done centuries before.

After two years of rebel warfare, a message came from Elizabeth, the queen of England. Gently scolding her naughty boys, she expressed "motherly" concern, "tearfully" queried their reasons for such misbehavior. Would the dear boys Hugh O'Neill and Red Hugh O'Donnell meet with her ambassadors to register their complaints against the English so that she could take steps to correct the problems?

"I know exactly what she has in mind. Too often I have watched while she has arranged for 'conferences' with those who get in the way of her wishes and interfere with her goals. It may be a gift of a bottle of fine wine, carefully flavored with her own special spices. But this time I believe she has a simpler method of eliminating troublesome 'boys.' We shall see."

"But she begs." young Red Hugh exulted. "We have brought the Queen herself to the table!"

"And where do you suppose the English will want to meet with us?" O'Neill responded. "Likely in some grand mansion where we will meet behind a locked door, never to be seen again. Perhaps it will be in a neatly walled town where the gates will be closed behind us forever and our heads decorating the corner posts, as was my uncle Shane O'Neill's. Shane's fate was made possible by a traitorous assassin. I know their tricks quite well. Too many times, honest, gullible folks have suddenly disappeared, never to bother the English anymore. Sure then, we will meet with them and state our case. But it will be out on an open meadow where no archers nor spearmen can hide in the groves. And we will meet them with our full armies of Irish standing in plain sight behind us, ready to attack if anything goes awry. The English deputies will indeed stand still and hear our demands which, of course, they will never agree to. In fact, I have a personal request, and I want to see the face of my enemy when I give it."

The meeting was arranged exactly as Hugh O'Neill directed. The night before the confrontation, Hugh held his lovely wife in his arms and grinned wickedly.

"We meet tomorrow with the queen's ambassadors," he said. "Surely, the grand marshal of all Ireland will be there, my love. I will state the demands of the Irish to stop our warring with them. I have a special demand to make from your brother, you know."

"Have you now?" Mabel asked. Then she suddenly realized what it would be. Her dowry, of course. She snuggled down into her husband's embrace contentedly. "I hope he has a stroke."

"My demands for our Irish freedom will sound logical and, to the Irish, perfectly realistic. I know that the English will refuse anyway, so I will make it easy for Henry Bagenal to refuse. The O'Donnell and I will continue to do righteous battle, and we will be the victors, no petty compromises with the English. And you, my duchess, my princess, when the Irish conquer and drive out the English usurpers, a new high king of Ireland will be chosen, and you will become my queen!"

Out on an open plain, the two armies rode slowly to meet. The leaders of the queen's army and the Irish chieftains faced one another. Gradually the officers rode forward until they could speak clearly to one another. Hugh O'Neill, the earl of Tyrone, and Red Hugh O'Donnell, the earl of Tirconnell, faced several arrogant deputies of Queen Elizabeth, among them Marshall Sir Henry Bagenal. The marshall demanded an accounting for the violent attacks against the Elizabethan planters.

"I have demands of my own," Hugh responded in a quiet, confident voice. "These they are: "Firstly, the English Protestants will cease to torture and kill Catholic priests and will allow Catholic people to worship in peace and safety. Secondly, the English may remain within the Pale, but all of the territory now occupied by Irish will remain in Irish possession and will not be under any kind of regulations by English marshals or sheriffs. We will maintain our own laws with our own officers."

Hugh paused. Irritated beyond control, Henry said, "Well, on with it! What other impossible demands will you make?"

A wide, wily smile crossed the face of the earl, delighted at the Englishman's ire.

"The last one is just for you," Hugh said. "Without complete compliance with these three demands there will be no peace in Ireland."

"Yes?" Henry demanded, impatient to get the farce over with.

"You will pay me the one thousand pounds you owe me for wedding the lady Mabel Bagenal, your sister, whom I raised to the dignity of being the bride of an O'Neill!"

～◎～

Mabel Bagenal O'Neill only had four years of happy marriage before she died, but she was married to the grand man of her own choice, a hero, a descendant of kings. Her dominant, conniving brother, Henry Bagenal, was killed by an Irish bullet at the Battle of Yellow Ford. Hugh O'Neill never became king of all Ireland. The Irish rebels were defeated at the Battle of Kinsale after nine years of hard-fought war against the English intruders.

George Bernard Shaw said, "Eternal is the fact that the human being born in Ireland and brought up in its air is Irish." Mabel Bagenal was an Irish colleen.

Maire Rua O'Brien, Red Mary

Elizabeth I died. After some furor among the kings of England, Oliver Cromwell became Protestant "Lord Protector of England" in 1646. He invaded predominantly Catholic Ireland, determined to totally eradicate that religion by genocide, which bloody purpose he very nearly succeeded in doing. He marched his army across the countryside, killing and burning. In place of wages for his army, which he could not afford, he awarded confiscated estates to officers. They took over, driving anyone they didn't kill out into the stony Burren of western Ireland.

Red Mary. She had a reputation for being strong willed, a formidable force to be reckoned with. She was.

It was in 1651 that Cromwell's army, under the control of Oliver Cromwell's son, Henry, continued the march across Ireland, burning churches and monasteries, murdering Catholic priests, monks, men, women, and children. Cromwell had gone back to England to continue his reign as Lord Protector of the Faith, "the faith" being Protestant. The troops led by officers in austere, black uniforms came more and more near to Clare, driving the Irish they had not killed into the stony hills of the west.

Maire and her husband, Conor O'Brien, had remodeled a tall Norman tower house in Clare, giving it paned windows, attractive gardens, and patrician doorsteps flanked by low stone walls. Green vines covered the right side of the building, which housed the servants and had only fifteenth century narrow slits for windows. The corner watch box still protruded from the third floor level, but the "murder hole" that sheltered and protected the main entry hall had been removed to reveal a beautiful arched doorway. The house and grounds were surrounded by low, dry-stone walls to keep the cattle and sheep from wandering in and devouring the flowers and shrubs.

Lemanagh Castle was a magnificent manor house in County Clare. The surrounding countryside was a pleasant location for it in the stony hills of Connaught. Conor O'Brien and Maire Rua and the six children were reasonably happy there. Maire's three older sons sired by her deceased first husband, Daniel Neylon O'Dea, no longer lived with her. Maire's temper, evidenced by her flaming red hair, which gave her the name of Maire Rua, Red Mary, occasionally flared up, and the household walked softly for a while.

The castle stood some miles north of Limerick town. Word came that the city was attacked by Cromwell's forces and the English army continued to march ominously toward Lemanagh.

Conor sent servants out to the rough farm cottages to bring the farmers into the grounds of the manor house to help defend it. He had never before seen the need to prepare an army strong enough to withstand the professional English soldiers and mercenary gallowglasses. Terrible fear for their families was in the faces of the farmers, and their voices were high-pitched with terror. They knew that the English soldiers were instructed to kill every Catholic man, woman, and child in Ireland. "Nits make gnats," Cromwell said.

While Conor deployed his rustic troops along the low stone walls, Maire sent their eldest son, thirteen-year-old Donough, to the watch nest on the upper corner of the house. They waited.

Suddenly Donough called out, "Cromwell's army is coming! I can see smoke on the other side of the Shannon!"

Immediately Maire ran down the stone steps from the third level to the large entrance hall, where Conor stood with his leaders.

"Cromwell's army is coming close!" she shouted, her brown eyes wide with alarm. "He is crossing the Shannon!"

"Here it comes, my lads," Conor said. "Send my warriors to slow them down at the bridge, but set everyone else at the stone walls around the house. Except for the house itself, those walls are our only defense! Get on now!"

Conor turned to his pretty, red-haired wife. "Maire, take all of our children to the fourth level. Arm the boys with muskets and pikes and hide Mary. I can't think how terrible it would be for her if Cromwell's soldiers found her. I wish your older sons were here. We will have to trust Donough to take charge."

Maire gave a sound of contempt. "It's no good they would be. Take after their father, they do. Let them stay with his people. Donough has better sense than the three of them put together. He and his four brothers will hold the house!"

"I hope they won't have to," Conor spoke almost in despair. "'Tis a fine, strong house, is this old tower house. It has good, stout stone walls, but I wish in our repairing, we had not torn down the murder hole. It would have been a blessing right now. Pray for our good men, Maire. Brave they are, but I don't know how they will fare against Cromwell's trained soldiers."

He gazed at his wife for a long minute. Eleven births she had had. Nine children still alive. Yet there was a vibrant beauty to her, a lively power and strength. Slim and pretty, she was, with her fiery mane of tresses, her large, brown eyes and very red lips. She wasn't old, only thirty-six. Instead of wearing on her, bearing children seemed to revitalize her. He reached for Maire and gave her a resounding kiss before dashing out the door to be with the desperate army of farmers.

Maire rushed up the stairs. She *hated* having Conor face that well-equipped, trained army. He was a good man, and a fine father for her brood. *Holy Mary, protect him,* was her frantic prayer. Shouting for Donough to come out of the watch nest, she called the young ones together on the top floor.

"Your father is gone out with his army to fight

Cromwell. You will stay up here. Hide your sister if the soldiers come. Use your good sense, Donough. Don't even let them know you are all up here if they break through into the house. The only things up here are old trunks and tools left from doing over the house. Your lives are the most important things to save!"

The young leader quickly placed his youthful troops in position at the small, fourth-floor windows, holding back to avoid being seen from below, while Maire hurried back down the steps.

Some of their men were posted inside the house, watching through the large, paned windows. Maire could see Conor outside walking behind the walls, encouraging the farmers.

The defenders knew well the dreadful reputation of Cromwell's army. Oliver Cromwell had made himself "Lord Protector"of England and Ireland. "Protecting" Ireland meant destroying everything Catholic and much that was not Catholic. He plied his fiery path across the island leaving horror and devastation behind. He warned all the peasantry to "Go to Hell or Connaught"—it was all the same. The stony western part of Ireland had "not enough water to drown a man, trees enough to hang him, nor earth enough to bury him in."

Conor O'Brien chose to hold fast and fight for his home and lands. The country folk stood with him, knowing they were outclassed as soldiers but determined to stake their lives on the hope of saving their homesteads and families.

The army came. Horsemen rode hard over the hill and bore down on the lone house standing behind low stone walls, hooves thundering while foot soldiers came running, screaming blood-curdling battle cries.

O'Brien ran among his men, hunched over behind the wall. The battle was on! The peasants held their ground while blood ran on both sides of the stones. Then Maire saw a man leave the ranks and come running toward the house.

"Stay there, you fool! Don't run away!" she shouted.

He paid no attention to her words and burst into the house. "You must come, Red Mary! Conor, he's been wounded!"

Conor?

She was out the door and flying down the grade toward the battle. Her brilliant red hair broke loose from its bands and flew out behind her. She found Conor tucked down behind the nearest wall. Blood covered the padded doublet over his chest. His face was gray. She pulled him into her arms. He barely had time to murmur, "Maire Rua, my love," before his head dropped back. He was dead.

Around her the clang of swords, the ugly thump of pikes in flesh, explosions of muskets, the insane screams of fury and pain raged on while Maire Rua O'Brien held her husband close in her arms, her tears mingling with his blood. Then she remembered, "The children!"

Rising, she ducked and tore away from the flailing weapons and ran to the house just as Cromwell's horsemen leaped over the wall. Inside the doors she looked with pity on the small band which was pledged to protect the house.

"Fight or flee, good men!" she ordered. "Do what you must for your own sakes!"

Up the stone staircase she went, petticoats flying beneath the heavy, blue linen skirt. As she went through the narrow opening where steps would take her to the fourth level, she yanked the old wooden door shut and threw the bar. At the upper level, she told her wide-eyed, frightened younger sons, Teige, Turlough, Murrough, and Honora, to get away from the windows where they might be seen. Donough was ready to run down the steps and join the clash of battle they could hear below. Maire forbid him.

The sounds of battle faded not soon enough, but they could hear the English soldiers on the floors below, ransacking, breaking, shouting crows of victory. Together Maire and Donough hid ten-year-old Mary behind an old chimney and piled dirty rags over her.

A long time later, the soldiers, carrying armloads of food and booty, trailed out of the house and made their way to re-form their ranks out on the lea. From the deep-set windows, the family watched them move away and follow their officers across the meadow and out of sight toward Limerick town.

As soon as darkness had fully set in, Maire and Donough crept down into the lower rooms. The house was a disaster. Everything that could be carried was gone. Everything else was broken or burned. They found the dead farmers strewn about, their bodies ravaged.

Maire and the young man slipped out into the dark and, by faint moonlight, they found Conor's body lying beneath the massacred bodies of two other defenders.

"'Tis good that they covered him, else those mad soldiers would have torn him to pieces and had his head on a pike. Let us get him to the house, my son, and give him a proper wake."

Conor O'Brien, descendant of the great Brian Boru, valiant defender of his home and family, lay in state on a table in the dining room of the house. The bodies of the hapless defenders had been dragged out into the yard by the O'Brien youths, their eyes wide with revulsion and horror as they did that which must be done. Then Conor's family stood around him in stunned silence. The entire nightmare of the day had left them shaken and exhausted.

"One more thing we must do," Maire said quietly. "Teige, you are quick on your feet for an eleven-year-old. I know you are weary, but I must ask you to go for a priest."

"*A priest?*" With Cromwell's Protestants offering a bounty for the head of any priest, Teige knew it would be his own death to be caught with one.

"It's dangerous, I know, but I will not have your father cast into an unhallowed grave to be forgotten. Go now. You know the high cairn along the way to Bunratty? If you look carefully under the heather, you'll be finding an opening dug into the side. My cousin, Father MacMahon, is hiding there. Bring him, and take no argument from him, do you hear? You'll be telling him that Red Mary wants him and he will come or be sorry!"

Maire and the rest of her children knelt on the floor around the table used for a bier. There were bits of broken candles about, but she did not dare to show a flicker of light. They murmured their rosaries until, one by one, the children slid down and fell asleep on the floor.

Maire's body was exhausted but too tense to give in. Her mind raced. Looking around at her children curled helplessly onto the floor, she realized that, if they were to live safely or live at all, it would be up to her. What did she have to offer in exchange for them? Nothing that the soldiers couldn't take with one slice of a sword. Where were the soldiers now? Likely still marching on other villages, burning, killing, stealing.

Perhaps not. When they left, they had moved off toward the south, carrying their booty. Possibly their leaders had wearied of blood and death for a while and taken their army back to Limerick to regroup and rest. Soon they would decide to whom of those who served best in the carnage of Lemanagh they would award the estate of Conor O'Brien. She had little or no time.

A glimmer of an idea began to form in her foggy, tired mind. Weak, depleted, her head began to droop and the thought faded.

The priest came. He gave the proper rites to the fallen Conor O'Brien. It was impossible for them to bury Conor in hallowed ground beside the burned-out monastery as should be, because Cromwell's soldiers were constantly on the lookout for parishioners sneaking in there to hold mass. In the darkness before the coming dawn, Father MacMahon quickly blessed a sheltered spot on the estate, and Conor was buried there by his children and his wife.

It was over. Father MacMahon slipped away to his hiding place under the stones of a gravesite. Maire took her young ones up the stairs to sleep again on the cold floor of the fourth story, the wooden door securely fastened.

She sat down against a wall and curled her feet up under her to think. Before long, the soldiers would return to Lemanagh to award her house and lands to one of their officers, the spoils of war and thievery from the Irish people. Maire and her children would have to escape to try to survive on the gray stone hills of the Burren. Something must be done.

Once again she trailed through her thoughts to find a solution. Her children should have the right to their father's estate, the house and lands. Even if the Cromwellians took it legally, she, being a woman, could not lay claim to it. She needed a solid lever, a factor that could not be moved.

What did she have to work with? There was no money to bribe, no gold or treasure to dicker with. What was hers that she could trade for a secure claim to her children's rights?

Looking around the dusty, junk-strewn storage room, her eyes lighted on a chest that sat in a sheltered corner. What was in that chest?

The very thing! Just what she needed to twist fate her way.

If it did not work, she might be raped, dragged through the streets and hanged for a spy. So be it. She had to give it a try.

"Donough, wake up!" she said. "You know that old cart that sits out decaying in the meadow? Yes, the one without a wheel. Likely Cromwell's thieving army has not taken it. Take your brothers out there and repair it before it gets too light outside. And find a horse to draw it, any horse. I know all of our fine mounts have been taken. *But find one!* Go! Mary, get yourself up and come with me. I'll be needing your help."

Maire hurried to the ancient chest covered with cob-webs and filth. When they lifted the heavy lid, Mary was amazed to see that it was lined with cedar wood and there were many well-preserved things inside.

Maire began to dig into the box and, at last, came up pulling out a large, rich red velvet gown. She shook it out.

"Why, it's beautiful!" Mary exclaimed.

"Indeed it is. 'Tis the gown I wore when first I met your father. I kept it, but we've had little enough social gatherings out here in Clare so I had no need of it. I need it now. Bring that white lace shawl there, and I be-lieve there is a long strand of pearls. Ah, there they are in that little leather bag. Let's be going downstairs to see what we can do with it all."

In her battered bedchamber on the second level of the house, Maire laid out the gown. Deep red velvet lay in huge, puffed sleeves and full, flowing skirt. The bodice was cut low. Delicate white lace fell crisply over the tops of the sleeves where they were attached to the dress and burst in sumptuous folds at the ends of the sleeves. A chain of golden circlets was attached to the waist.

"We must hurry, Mary child. See if you can find my hair brush in all this broken and ripped-up mess."

Before long, Maire Rua O'Brien stood in the room gloriously gowned in pearls and gold and rich velvet. Her vibrant red hair was brushed and braided around her head leaving the back billowing around her shoulders.

"Tell me, Mary, do I look well? I must look wealthy and refined."

"Sure, my mam, you look as grand as a queen. It's

hard for me to believe that you are the mother who rules our house and looks after the boys and me."

"I hope you see it true, Mary, for I don't want to look like a woman who was married twice and who has borne eleven children."

"Why, Mam? What are you planning?"

"One way or another, you will find out soon enough."

In a little while, Donough appeared to announce that the cart was repaired and a pony was found wandering by the Shannon.

"I feared it was wild, one of those descended from those loosed by the Spaniards when they shipwrecked the Spanish Armada. But someone has trained it well. It is hitched to the cart."

Maire breathed a deep sigh which, by the way, caused her bosom to swell even more above the low-cut bodice. The eyes of her sons widened and Donough frowned with suspicion.

"What would you be up to now, Maire Rua? I'm not liking the looks of this."

She turned on him angrily. "I'm going to save your inheritance, Donough O'Brien! I'm going to save the lives of my children. It's not of your concern how I'm to do it. Bring that wolfskin off the floor and cast it over the seat of the cart. I will be off to Limerick." Seeing his next question in his eyes, she said, "You'll not go with me. *I go alone!*"

Tossing the white lace shawl around her head and shoulders, she climbed onto the hostler's seat of the cart and began the drive south to Limerick town.

Soldiers were everywhere in the town. Their tattered

clothing and sinister, dusty, black hats told the story of their deadly killing march, months of ugly carnage. There was a look about them of wild animals who had tasted blood and lost any respect for human life. Inwardly, Maire trembled but was not going to let fear stop her mission.

She saw the standard of Protestant England hung above the door of a stone Catholic church, apparently commandeered for army headquarters. A pair of guards stood on the street and she hailed them.

"You there, you lazy louts! Have you lost your manners? Get yourselves here and help a lady down."

Startled at her audacity, they quickly came and assisted her properly off the cart.

Then she marched smartly into the church without hesitating.

The church foyer had been changed into an office where several officers in their white-collared uniforms lounged.

"Don't be staring at me like a bunch of sheep." Maire demanded. "I want to speak to your commander."

One of the officers stood leaning against the wall in a clean, black wool uniform, crisp white cambric collar and shining knee-high boots. His long hair was tawny and his blue eyes studied Maire, carefully evaluating her appearance. He grinned, bemused at the pretty, red-haired woman who so brazenly made demands.

"I will be happy to call him," he said.

In seconds, he came out with a tall, gray-haired gentleman also wearing Puritan black.

"What is this? What are you after, young woman?"

"I'm here to get a husband for myself. I want you to

assign an officer to marry me!"

Every eye in the room went wide with shock.

"A husband, is it? Are you mad, woman?"

"Perhaps I am. Perhaps your army has deprived me of every good man in Ireland and I will not go on unmarried!"

Stumbling, the commander asked, "A fine lady like you, are you not married?"

"I am not."

She was not. Conor O'Brien lay under the cold earth of Clare.

"Yes, you are mad. I see that clearly now. Like all the Irish, you are headstrong and ignorant of proprieties. Shame! As if any one of my fine officers would be fool enough to marry a mad woman!"

"I believe I would."

They turned to look at the grinning officer who had brought out the commander.

"John Cooper, have you also gone mad?" the commander shouted.

Cooper stood up straight and strolled over to take a closer look at Maire. "I like her looks," he said. "She's a beauty, she is. And it's plain to see from her attire that she is not poor or ignorant. I like her spunk. I'll marry her, and be glad to do it."

The commander was near to speechless. He stuttered, "I have never heard of such a thing. What of your obligations to Cromwell?"

"I believe I have served him long enough and well enough that I should be able to retire. I will go home with this lady, wherever home may be, and settle down to married life."

After much argument from the commander and all of his fellow officers in the room, a Protestant chaplain was called and the marriage was performed.

"Come with me now, Husband," Maire said. "I must be getting home."

"I will get my horse."

It's done, Maire thought with relief. My children's home and lands would have been confiscated by Cromwell and given to one of his officers. But, as my husband, this officer will already possess them, and I possess him. My children's lives and property are secure.

Within hours, they were moving over the hills and crossing streams to Lemanagh Castle. When they came in sight of the big house, Cooper was startled and asked, "Is this your home?"

"It is."

"Are you a member of the O'Brien clan, then?"

"I am the mistress of Lemanagh Castle."

"I understood that O'Brien had a wife and many children?"

"So he had. But he is dead, killed by your army."

John Cooper was amazed but still amused. "So you were indeed single when you came to Limerick. And how many children have you?"

"Three sons by Daniel Neylon O'Dea, my first husband. Eight children by Conor O'Brien, but two of my daughters died of the plague deliberately brought into Ireland on contaminated blankets by the English."

"Nine children alive! Unbelievable! You are young and too pretty to have had eleven children!"

"It's thirty-six years old, I am. Married first when I

was fifteen to a man chosen by my father. He died. I am strong and healthy, and it seems I cannot help but be on the nest almost yearly."

Cooper was stunned into silence. He sat on his horse staring at the tall, stately walls of the ancient tower house turned into a mansion. It seems he had been tricked into a marriage of convenience by this amazing Irish woman.

However, fortune was good to him after all. She brought to him a dowry of a fine house and an estate of many acres of land. And nine children! He stared at the wife who had captivated and captured him. Her slim figure bloomed into a full bosom and she had tempting lips. Sure then, this lovely red head he had married was a good breeder and was certain to present him with children of his own.

He burst out into a hearty laugh. "Well now, Maire O'Dea O'Brien Cooper, I accept my fate. Perhaps I rushed into this alliance too quickly, but I'll not complain. You have made me a wealthy man of house and lands. Let's have a look at that brood of yours and see what kind of fine children I can expect to beget!"

～ஒ～

Red Mary's plan was successful. Cooper was an agreeable man and before he knew it he had signed an agreement to allow Donough O'Brien to inherit all of his father's properties, house and lands and all. It was done before Cooper's own two children were even anticipated. But John Cooper took it in his stride and, from his seat as master of Lemanagh, he speculated in the markets and built a fortune of his own.

Maire Rua performed her wifely duties, but there was no grand love between them, just a good-natured, tacit understanding that both would and did profit from their marriage.

Years later, Donough O'Brien moved the family seat from the damaged house at Lemanagh to Dromoland Castle, where Red Mary's portrait hangs today among the heroes of the O'Brien clan.

Sarah Curran, a Patriot's Love

In the eighteenth century, England established the "Penal Laws," under which no Catholic Irishman could own property, operate a business, be educated, or hold public office. Almost all of the native population of the island lived in stone hovels with mud floors, tenant farmers to the Anglo-Irish landlords.

In 1798, an uprising occurred. Clumsy Irishmen with homemade pikes and knives rebelled against the British control. Quickly, with the help of insidious informers, the effort was soon quelled. Masses of Irish people suffered indiscriminate torture and hangings for their "treason."

But, five years later, in the hearts of true Irishmen, the hope of freedom still lived.

Rath Castle in County Wicklow was ablaze with light on that May evening. Music filled the great hall from the strings hidden behind a portiere. Delicacies for the palate were heaped upon a long, white table along with flowers and gleaming candelabra. Ladies in the latest pastel, Empire-style gowns fluttered amid flattering gentlemen in their elegant black cutaways, tall collars, and slim trousers. And it was all for her.

Sarah Curran, only seventeen years old, stood nervously in the receiving line, gazing in awe at the wonderful ball given in her honor at the urging of her dear friend, Moira Lambart. For her part, Moira was delighting in the occasion. She stood next to Sarah, whispering. "It's so grand, my dear. You deserve such an honor, living as you do in Dublin with that old curmudgeon of a father and your siblings. I'm so glad I talked Papa into presenting you."

Moira caught Sarah's blue eyes focused on a group of gentlemen in a corner listening to a rather short but dominant man with dark eyebrows accenting his words. It was the lawyer John Philpot Curran regaling a group of prosperous gentlemen with his wit and clever remarks.

"Don't worry about your father, dear," Moira said. "He is too busy being the greatest attorney in Ireland to scold and intimidate you tonight. This is your night and you will enjoy it if I have to have him trussed up and hung in the stable until it's over."

A tiny smile tugged at Sarah's pink lips at her friend's brash threat. She carefully brushed her hand upward on her silky, golden hair, which had been joyfully curled and styled in the latest fashion by Moira for the grand evening. How lovely it would be if her mother were there to share her pleasure. But her mother had left the overbearing husband and all the children when Sarah was very young, and now lay cold in Newmarket cemetery. In her soft, white muslin gown tucked under her bosom and flowing to the floor, the tiny puffed sleeves and long white gloves, Sarah was the epitome of elegance. But the modest manner in which she watched the affair proved that she was no fashion plate snob.

After Sarah shyly turned down three hopeful young men who offered their arms to dance, Moira became impatient. "The next bright young fellow who comes will be your dance partner, and I'll take no resistance from you, my pretty friend," she declared. "Ah now, here comes a tempting catch. And do you see the look of glory on his face at the sight of you? Get yourself ready to be fawned over, my girl."

He was indeed a handsome boy, his black silk cravat wrapped and neatly tied above his waistcoat, and his slim trousers pencil thin to the top of his shining black pumps. But there was a boyish delight in his eyes as they rehearsed the sight of the lovely maiden.

"Robert Emmett at your service, Miss Lambart," he bowed elaborately to Moira. "May I be introduced to this lady?"

"You may." Moira took pains to be certain that her little friend was soon on the dance floor, mincing, posturing, and bowing to the music of the strings under the adoring eyes of Mr. Emmett.

To Moira Lambart's delight, the introduction did not stop with one dance. Robert clung to his sudden infatuation throughout the whole party. At his leaving, he gazed longingly at Sarah Curran.

"May I have your permission to call on you, Miss Sarah?" he ventured, his amorous feelings making him bold.

"Perhaps not," she answered quietly. "I believe my father would not allow it."

"Your father, Barrister Philpot? Why, I believe he might allow it after all. He and my father are quite good friends, you know. Surely, I would be welcome to call upon him and, if you happen to be at home, then I may see you, may I not? I'll be in Dublin at Trinity College, not too far from The Priory, where your family resides. It will be grand!"

The boy was delighted with his solution to the situation, so delighted that he didn't notice the look of dismay in Sarah's soft blue eyes. He left the house on winged feet, confident that he would see her again soon.

Later, as Sarah and Moira sat curled up on the chaise in Moira's bedroom, they chatted over the events of the wonderful evening.

"Oh, Sarah, I can't get over how quickly that dear boy, Robert Emmett, fell for you. He is so happy that you will be close to Dublin so he may call."

Sarah's eyes became troubled. "Really, Moira, I wish you wouldn't encourage him. He is a nice enough young man, but if he takes to coming to our home too often Father may realize what he is doing and become angry."

"That is solved, too," Moira exulted. "Before he left we talked. When he cannot get away from college, he will send you letters."

"Letters! Oh, he mustn't. Father would read them and be furious at his audacity."

"We knew that, so we have a plan. Robert will send his 'love letters' to you through me."

Sarah moaned, "Oh, Moira, I'm truly not interested in him. He is rather childish. So full of boyish enthusiasm. So sure that I will fall in love with him."

"Maybe you will." Moira laughed. "I hope so."

Sure enough, Robert Emmett began dropping by the Curran house occasionally as often as he could get away from his books. Mr. Curran was flattered. The two gentlemen were both nationalists, members of the United Irish Society. Robert's brother was Thomas Addis Emmett, one of the principle leaders of the Rising of 1798. They often discussed Ireland's efforts to break away from England, and Robert sincerely expressed his admiration for the barrister's defense of United Irishmen in the courtroom.

In his concentration with his own self interests, John P. Curran barely noticed the minutes when Robert caught Sarah alone in the garden or in the hallway, a quiet word here, a loving look there. The young man reveled in every second of attention from her that he could glean.

And there were letters, many letters. They came encased in packets from Moira, supposedly messages from her loving girlfriend at Rath Castle in Wicklow. But the sealed, small envelopes inside the larger ones held words of love and adoration, pleading with her to return his love and give him an opportunity to approach her father.

One day Sarah arrived home just as Robert was leaving the house. She wished she could hide her face inside her long bonnet and not have to speak to him, but he would not have it that way. With the house door closed behind him, it was not unseemly for the two to converse on the front steps.

"Sarah, my love," he teased. "I was afraid I would not see you today and my heart would be broken."

Sarah shook her head. "Robert, I wish you would stop all of this. I do not love you. Please don't torment yourself . . . and *me* . . . calling continually and sending those embarrassing letters. *Please!*"

He smiled. "You don't believe you love me, but you will. I love you too much to go away and forget you. I am graduating from Trinity and going to Paris to visit my brother, Thomas, and you will miss me. I will come again as soon as I get back. And this time, I will get your father's permission to call on *you!* You will see that my love for you is so strong, you will learn to love me."

Sarah turned away and let herself in the door to the fine home ruled by her father. As she shut the door on the happy, confident face of Robert Emmett, she shook her head. He was really a dear, gentle boy, only twenty-two years old. There was something truly likeable in that narrow face, with the tender, sensitive mouth and bright, ardent eyes. His letters were sweet, but full of impractical dreams and desires.

Perhaps she would miss him. But the idea that such a young fellow who had no particular fortune or profession would appeal to her father made the whole concept impossible. Why she kept that bundle of little letters in her bureau drawer, she didn't know. Someday maybe they would make a pleasant memory.

At the insistence of his father, Robert went to Europe on the Grand Tour. He came back home a year later, filled with patriotic zeal inspired by his exiled brother.

Thomas Addis Emmett had narrowly missed the gallows after the Rising of '98, and had settled in France, contemplating a trip to America to raise support for the United Irishmen. He had been negotiating with Napoleon for support of a new rebellion of Ireland against the British rule. The self-styled emperor made grand promises of troops and money to the United Irishmen if a new insurrection was made. The French leader was pleased to annoy his wartime enemies in England by offering to help Ireland break free. Thomas and the rest of the displaced United Irishmen were overjoyed, certain that this time they would come forth the victors. He sent Robert back to Dublin ready to call the rebels together again.

The letters kept coming while he was on the Continent, letters full of hope and passion for Ireland's freedom. Sure then, Sarah and the Currans, the Emmetts, and many other Protestant professional Irish lived in comfort and plenty, but her father often deplored the fields and estates which were teeming with Catholic peasants living in the most awful poverty. Like slaves they were, for they worked hard for only the privilege of living in stone huts with dirt floors. They worked the Protestant Anglo's farms and, through the long, wet winters, subsisted on tiny patches of potatoes and cabbages. In Dublin town, she saw grimy, cold children living in ghettos, sick, starving people who had been evicted from their huts to make room for the rich men's cattle. If Robert cared to free those poor, destitute people, then Sarah saw him in a different light. He was worthwhile, not just a playboy student. Slowly she began to feel a tender affection for the rambunctious rebel. Letters began to flow in both directions now, keeping Moira Lambart excited and happy, sure that soon the two would come together in a flourishing marriage.

With unspeakable, youthful zeal, Robert Emmett went to work in Ireland, organizing a new uprising of the United Irishmen. He traveled across Ireland, rounding up an army of willing rebels. Hope grew in the oppressed people, hope tempered with cautious realism because of memories of the all too recent horrors of defeat only five years before in 1798. But the memories of punishing atrocities by the yeomen of Ulster and the British generals also stirred a deep hate and fury in the poor of the land.

Sarah read the precious letters describing his success. Sometimes he wrote that he didn't even need to recruit men. It was almost *uncanny* how they came to him of their own accord, stepping right into the thick of the plans. He was filled with exhilarating pride in his successful raising of contingents, bodies of farmers and homeless men waiting for his order to march on Dublin Castle, that bastion of English control.

Deep in the Wicklow Mountains, he came upon Michael O'Dwyer and his band of insurrectionists still hiding in caves. O'Dwyer was a seasoned rebel and wary of the plan, but ready to join any efforts to break England's control of Ireland. His troops stood ready to come at Robert Emmett's command.

Robert pulled the scheme together. He gathered guns and powder and hand weapons and had them stashed in houses around Dublin. Groups of United Irishmen in the counties of Carlow, Wexford, Kildare, and Wicklow were also standing ready for the assault on Dublin Castle when the French sent their supporting troops, likely in late July, 1803.

On July 16, Daniel, one of Robert's men, slipped into his quarters in a Dublin hotel and whispered, "Robert boyo, something is gone amiss. The guns and powder, all the ammunition we had stored on Patrick Street is gone, blown to pieces!"

Robert jumped up. Looking out the window, he could see the street filling with people chattering about the grand explosion. Soldiers were pouring down the southward streets toward St. Patrick's cathedral and Patrick Street.

"How did it happen? Who knew where the stash was and would destroy it?" Robert wailed in a whisper.

"I'm not knowing, lad, but I'm thinking we'd better think over our plan. It's sure the British are aware of our doings and they will catch us all for the hangman's rope. Let's call it off and lie low for a while."

"Call it off?" Robert's face went numb. It was his whole life! All of his love of books and peace had been rolled up to live later, after he had led his country to freedom. And Sarah, he loved her so much and wanted to make her proud.

Daniel's voice went firm. "Call it off, Robert. The signs are clear. If you keep on with it, it's sure you'll die!"

Robert began to doubt that his organization was secure. But everything was set. The French were supposed to arrive at a later date, but he saw that things were going awry.

"Perhaps we should make our move quickly," he said. "If the British have an idea that we are going to strike, perhaps we will catch them off guard."

"Take my word for it, lad. If they know anything, they know it all. Run for your life, son! That's exactly what I'm doing," Daniel said and slipped warily out the door and out of sight.

That night Robert Emmett, gentle and thoughtful man that he truly was, appeared in the stable of The Priory. A stableboy found Sarah choosing a book from the well-stocked shelves in the library and slipped a message into her hand. She hurried through the servant's door to meet her lover. For the first time, she rushed into his arms.

"My darling, my Robert. I'm so glad to see you, to touch you! It has been so long. The letters have been wonderful, but not enough!"

Robert withdrew from her joyful embrace. His eyes were troubled and his face pale and solemn. "Sarah, dear love. I had to see you to tell you that it is over between us." He paused, his voice quiet and strained. "The English know that we have gathered guns and fighting men for a new insurrection. I am a wanted man. I cannot offer you a life. In fact, I must leave the country right away!"

Sarah was stunned. "Leave? But you said everything was in place. All your men are ready to fight for Ireland. You are going to lead the United Irish to victory. I know you can. Oh, my dearest Robert, you can do it!"

Robert put his arms around her and kissed her soft, pink lips. Then he pushed her gently away. "You don't understand how it is. I was a fool. I trusted everyone. The ranks of my army are saturated with spies and informers. The English know about it all. The Lord Deputy has simply let the plans go forward, waiting until we make our move. *I must run.* No longer can I offer you hope that I will be a man of position, that we could marry and make a home together. But I could never leave the country without seeing you once more and telling you goodbye. This is the end for us. Forget me. Let your father find a good man for you who will give you the things you deserve to have. Goodbye, Sarah Curran, my love." His voice revealed great distress.

"Robert, no!" Sarah threw her arms around him and clung to his slim, young shoulders. "I won't let you leave me! I won't let you give up!"

"Sarah, don't you see. I was a fool. I trusted people too much. I'm not a warrior."

"Robert, my love, I know your heart. You love our country and hate the tyranny that the poor people live under. Don't lose everything you have planned and worked for. You have men. You have weapons. You are a fine man, a leader."

Suddenly Robert Emmett stood taller. Sarah *believed* in him.

"Do you truly believe I can do it, Sarah? Do you think that I can be the one to set Ireland utterly free of English rule?"

"I believe it!" she declared. "Robert, you are a wonderful man. I have read your letters and seen how you inspire your troops. I have learned to love you." She reached up to touch his face. "I cannot lose you, not now. Above all, please, Robert, don't leave me. I couldn't bear to have you gone and never see you again."

Tears welled up in her blue eyes, and his heart became tender. Pride lighted his eyes. A confident smile broke through the despair on his face.

"Sarah, you make me strong. I will do it! Only wait now, my only love, until the battle is over and we have won. Then I will come back. Your father will be proud of me, and I will ask him to allow me to marry you. My beloved!" Then he held her and kissed her, thrilled at her willing response. Finally, in the dark of the night, he slipped away. He would raise the rebellion. He would win, and he would return for her, she knew it.

Two days later, Sarah heard the news.

There never was a battle. Somehow, no doubt through British networking, Robert's army did not come. He sent word to the Kildare troop. Someone told them to turn back. Orders were funneled to Carlow and Wexford. They were not received. Michael O'Dwyer and his band in the Wicklows waited but never were called.

Two thousand Dublin men were expected to be ready to march on Dublin Castle. About eighty appeared, drunken rabble from the ghetto, armed with pikes and clubs.

Young Robert Emmett stood in the dark streets of the city, uncertain, distressed.

Someone shouted, "The army is coming! They're almost here!"

"Very well," he said, pulling an old sword out of its scabbard. "Very well, let's march!"

He led his unruly gang down the streets toward the castle. Around a corner came a lone carriage. The men, excited and ready to begin action, surrounded the carriage and dragged the elderly Chief Justice, Lord Kilwarden, and his nephew into the street and piked them to death.

That was the final disaster. The blood of the old man that spread across the cobblestones horrified the young man who had thought to lead a righteous army to fight armed soldiers. Robert Emmett dispersed the bloodthirsty, riotous mob and took himself out of sight.

Sarah listened to the tale as her father ranted, and she felt a sickness overwhelm her. It would seem that Robert was right, he should have dropped the effort and left for the sake of his life. What would happen now? Could he get away yet?

Dear God, please keep him safe. If he has escaped to a safe place, make him go ahead and get out of Ireland! I will meet him anywhere he wants. I should never have urged him to try it. I didn't know how it was!

The morning after the botched insurrection, John Philpot Curran found a detachment of soldiers on his doorstep. Major Sirr informed him politely that they had orders to search his home for evidence regarding the trouble the night before. "You being a nationalist, sir, and the rumor that one in your family was well acquainted with the instigator of the trouble."

"Indeed you may search my home, without question," Curran responded. "I have nothing at all to hide. I was not involved in any way, and you are welcome to prove it otherwise."

He did not notice the grayed face of his daughter

who stood listening to the conversation. Sarah left and went to the garden where she collapsed on a stone bench and wept. So long she had held Robert Emmett's love at bay. Now that he was her hero, her brave patriot, she would surely lose him one way or another. She prayed that he would go away, that he would not be arrested to face the horrors of a British execution.

She could hear the noise of the soldiers searching the house. Then the sound of her father's voice raised in anger. Steps clicked on the stone walk of the garden. Her father appeared before her. In his hands he held a packet of white letters.

"What does this mean?!" His face was red and his eyes wide with fury.

She bowed her head. "I love Robert Emmett."

"You *love* him? When did all this come about? You have been deceiving me!"

She lifted her head then, her reddened eyes at last bold to her father. "You would never have understood. You would have kept us apart. I had to keep silent about my love for him."

"Indeed I would have. He is nothing but a dreamer without ambition or income. I would have put a stop to such foolishness. Now it is too late. These letters," Curran ranted. "He told you everything he was doing. I am a loyal United Irishman, but you didn't see fit to let me know about them. This makes it appear that I supported his wild schemes to attack Dublin Castle!"

"You would have turned him in to the English."

"Indeed I would! He is a silly young fool to think he could have led an insurrection. Men would have died, as indeed poor old Kilwarden did. He had not the brains to do it. And he had not the right to bring you into it!"

"He was following his heart and his love for Ireland."

"And showing off for you, he was. Imbecile! Fool! I promise you that you will never see him again. He was never fit to bring suit for the daughter of John Philpot Curran."

"I pray you never find him."

"We will. He has sent another letter to you. It came just now. He says he must see you once more before he escapes. When he gets to Harold's Cross, Major Sirr will be waiting for him. The major will arrest a woman by the name of Anne Devlin, also. Emmett's letter says she is the niece of Michael O'Dwyer, the outlaw. No doubt she has harbored Emmett before, and she is in the thick of it."

Sarah covered her face with her trembling hands, agonizing for Robert. Then a thought came to her, a tiny thread of hope.

"Father," she pleaded, "you can *defend* Robert in court. You have defended United Irishmen before. The courts have respect for you. They will listen."

"You are out of your mind, Sarah Curran. Don't you realize that your outrageous behavior has put my reputation on the line? I shall be investigated. Embarrassed beyond words. Defend Robert Emmett? I will not even see him until he stands in the dock before English judges. And I will applaud his conviction of high treason!"

With that, he charged out of the garden, still clutching the incriminating letters. Sarah sat still on the cold, stone bench, slowly seeing the picture of all that had come about. In her eyes, she saw that those letters may not have been written if her father was not such an overpowering tyrant, keeping her and all his children in tight-fisted constraints. How different it might have been if Robert had been allowed to court her openly. Perhaps he would not have been such an easy pawn for the survivors of '98 to use to start a new insurrection if she and he had been moving forward to a life together.

And she saw clearly just how her own selfish desires figured in the horrible disaster that fell on the soft, loving heart of Robert Emmett. She had encouraged him to be a hero, to make a name for himself, so she could be proud. But more powerful than all of her other motives had been her fear that he would go away to France or America and she would lose him forever. The thought sent her into panic when she finally realized how much she really loved him. She had begged him not to leave and he, in his love for her, thrilled at her request. Now he would surely go away forever, likely to his doom.

She staggered weakly to her feet and, shaking, made her way into the house and to her own bedchamber.

Robert, caught at Harold's Cross, was swiftly taken to Dublin Castle, a place where few prisoners ever left alive and, if alive, left in savagely brutalized condition. Michael O'Dwyer's niece was thrown in Kilmainham Gaol and released two years later with her health broken from the cold, dehumanizing circumstances.

From his cell in Dublin Castle, Robert sent a last letter, this time to John Philpot Curran. Curran waved the paper at Sarah's face.

"See here. *Now* he is contrite. He apologizes for

doing me 'severe injury' which even his life cannot atone for, he says. He says he has offered to plead guilty if his shameful letters to you will be kept out of it. He says that, if he could change things, he would devote his life to making you happy. Silly, foolish rot! Too late!"

"Did he ask you to defend him?" Sarah asked.

"He did. I received that letter days ago. Now he says he knew I would not, but it would look strange to the authorities if he did not ask me since I have defended many other insurrectionists. He was right indeed. I would rather defend the demons in Hell than touch that witless young fool's case."

"I was certain you wouldn't," Sarah said in a wooden tone. She walked silently from the room, leaving her father to fume and curse the man she loved.

Robert Emmett was tried before a British court September 19, 1803. At his sentencing, he clutched at his final opportunity to speak, to bring forth his proud purpose. The courtroom was crowded with lords and soldiers. From a seat far back in the gallery, a veiled and silent young woman listened.

Standing in the dock box, surrounded by upright sharp spikes, Robert's voice carried across the space to the elevated dais where stern, white-wigged judges sat. He told the court that he knew nothing he could say would change their prejudiced minds.

"The man dies, but his memory lives. That mine may not perish, that it may live in the respect of my countrymen, I seize upon this opportunity to vindicate myself. . . ."

He said that he was less afraid of the scaffolds *"since sentence was already pronounced at the castle, before your jury was impaneled"* than that he would be remembered as only a criminal, that some day brave Irish patriots would accomplish that which he had set out to do.

In her corner of the gallery, Sarah wept silently. In her heart she was proud of her beloved, proud of his staunch patriotism. But why should Robert Emmett, gentle, bookish boy that he was, give his life for his country when he should have years before him? She knew the answer. His life was all he had to give now. His life and her happiness must be sacrificed.

One of the judges, Lord Norbury, interrupted him, demanding that he should not have to sit there and listen to treason, but Robert pounded on, determined to leave behind more than just a ravaged and dismembered body and a reputation for being a scoundrel.

He was accused of being a traitor, selling out his country to France for ambition. With truthful clarity he defended his position, pointing out that with his family background, he could easily have risen in the ranks of upper-class Englishmen and been among the oppressors of his people.

"I swear by the throne of Heaven . . . by the blood of the murdered patriots who have gone before me, that my conduct has been through all this peril, and all my purposes . . ." were the *"emancipation of my country from the superinhuman oppression under which she has so long and too patiently travailed. . . . I acted as an Irishman, determined on delivering my country from the yoke of a foreign and unrelenting tyranny . . . a government which is steeled to barbarity by the cries of the orphans and the tears of the widows which it has made."*

Judge Norbury interrupted once more, ordering Robert Emmett to be silent so they could pronounce his sentence. Robert protested that he only had one more thing to say. He wanted no one to write him an epitaph on his tombstone. At this point in time, anyone who wrote kindly of him would be arrested as a traitor. Someday, when Ireland was free, then it could be written truthfully.

"When my country takes her place among the nations of the earth, then, and not till then, let my epitaph be written!"

In the customary civilized manner of the British laws, Robert Emmett was legally executed. He was first hanged, strangled until almost dead. Then he was cut down and his head severed from his body with a blow of the axe. The executioner then proudly paraded back and forth across the platform, his bloody axe still in hand and the head dangling from his fist by a wad of hair. Blood gushed from the neck onto the boards while the crowd roared its approval and delicate ladies, who had come to view the entertainment, fainted. The head was properly sent along to have a death mask made, which would bring a fine reward to the sculptor.

John Philpot Curran returned home from the execution to find Sarah packing her clothes. The satisfaction in his eyes was replaced with surprise.

"Now then, what do you think you are doing?" he demanded.

"I'm leaving your house." She calmly continued to place her things into a trunk, not looking at her father.

"You will not!" he roared. "You will remain in my house and marry decently when I choose that you should. I will not be intimidated by my own daughter who has caused me trouble enough."

Sarah stopped packing. She stood up as tall as her delicate bones would allow. No tears filled her eyes. No blush of fear colored her white cheeks. Cold, controlled fury flashed from her blue eyes.

"It's leaving this house, I am! You have taught me to hate you, and I'm finding grand satisfaction in the feeling. You might have saved Robert from death. But, because he loved me, because you were embarrassed that I loved him, you refused to defend him. I can no longer bear the sight of you! I'll not spend one more minute in this house under your tyranny. I pity my brothers and sisters who must stay here. Get out of my sight."

Unbelievably, the great orator Curran could not speak. He had never imagined that one of his overpowered, dominated children would defy him, least of all tender little Sarah. He could see that, unless he would bodily deter her, she would be leaving his house. Stunned, he left the room.

Before long, the butler passed through the main hall carrying her luggage to a waiting coach. Sarah, dressed in bonnet and cloak, followed him and, without one more word to her father, left The Priory forever.

∼◎∽

The Penrose family, Quakers who lived in Cork, took her in gladly. They loved Sarah Curran, as everyone did, and tried their best to bring her out of her sorrow and despair.

Finally, Captain Richard Sturgeon, an officer of the Royal Staff Corps, fell in love with her. He courted her with passion and would not be denied the opportunity to make her happy.

She married him in 1806. He took her away to Italy, hop-

ing that the change would erase her memories and she could be happy. Sarah was a good wife to the captain, looking after his needs dutifully. Then one day she happened onto a painting of Robert Emmett standing in the dock before the cold British court.

Sarah's face went white. All the memories of her love, all the horrors of his fate, came crushing back. In the spring of 1808, Sarah Curran left this world to join her beloved somewhere in eternity.

Mary O'Connor, the Rose of Tralee

The great Daniel O'Connell had brought
about the Catholic Emancipation in *1831*,
allowing certain rights to that group of Irish.
However, the Protestant landlords and
wealthy tradesmen of the country maintained
a stigma on the Catholics, keeping them in
servitude. Tenant farmers grew grain crops to
pay the rents on their tiny, stone houses and
garden plots, where they grew potatoes, their
only source of food for the entire year. The
English Parliament paid little attention to the
ugly blight that swept across Ireland in *1845*,
turning healthy green potato plants and the fat
underground tubers into black, stinking slime.

A young man in the uniform of the British army
rode into Tralee, County Kerry, in April, 1849. His
skin was bronzed by the unrelenting sun of India, where
he had served the past four years. William Pembroke
Mulchinock rode slowly, trying to sort out his thoughts

and emotions. Forcing aside the recent memories and impressions of the faraway land, he gratefully drew back on thoughts of his life and his love before he was taken away from Ireland.

In all those seeming endless days in India, he hated having been conscripted into the army. He was sure that it was a scheme engineered by his mother to take him away from his sweet Mary. And how he hated the foreign country. The blazing sun, the nauseating smells of teeming humanity and filth in the streets and rivers. The everlasting taste of strange spices in the food.

And the terrible, merciless caste system. Around the walls of the finest palaces in the world, dwelling places of the Brahmin emirs, the pariahs lay in starvation and disease. The pariahs were the lowest of the low, the throwaway people, their only hope was of being reincarnated into a higher level of humanity in the next life. The brutality was unspeakable.

He had clung to thoughts of his beloved Ireland with its cool, green glens and soft rain showers that became rainbows. Forced to serve as a correspondent in the war, he was obliged to write of the roar of cannons and guns and bloodshed. He was a soldier by law but a poet at heart, and often when he was alone, he set down on paper beautiful, melodic memories and dreams of his Mary and his lush, beautiful homeland.

> *"In the far fields of India, 'mid wars dreadful*
> *thunders,*
> *Her voice was a solace and comfort to me."*

But his memories suffered appalling blows as he

traveled home on the roads and boreens from Dublin to Tralee in County Kerry on the western side of the island. Where were the pretty, rosy-cheeked children of the tenant farmers with their bright smiles? Where were the little cows and pigs and fat hens beside the tiny thatched stone cottages? In fact, what had happened to most of the cottages?

The sights he saw were incredible! Most cottages were destroyed and lay in piles of rubble. The families had been driven out and into the roads, their farmsteads growing up in weeds, while in the fields nearby grazed cattle, horses, and sheep. He saw those families huddled in ditches, begging for a little food, instead of contentedly going about their chores in the streetyards of their small homes. He passed workhouses, bare buildings surrounded by crowds of grasping, pleading skeletal people begging to get in for food.

Worse was the sight of hundreds of poor emaciated bodies of people crawling, stumbling, or lying still along the roads and byways, starved to death. No strange foreign country, this. It was Ireland, his home, the land he loved! How could this horror have happened?

The Famine, they called it. The Great Hunger. The potato crop had turned to black slime from a strange new enemy called "blight." The people could not eat from the fields of grain or of the fat cattle in the green meadows. Shiploads of corn and wheat, casks of butter and cheese, cured hams, all the produce of the country raised by the calloused hands of the tenant farmers, went across the water to be sold for the benefit of the landowners. Those things belonged to the Ascendancy, the wealthy absentee landlords who lived comfortably in another country on the revenue of that produce.

The gentle heart of William Mulchinock, the poet, staggered at the terrible sights. He was anxious to get home, to the pleasant town of his youth, to the fine house where he grew up playing on green lawns among lovely flowers. Surely, somehow all of this horror and unbelievable travesty would come together to make sense.

And most of all, he wanted to see his Mary. Memories of her wide, dark eyes, her fair skin, the way she tossed her shining brown hair, those beautiful images had kept his sanity on long, stifling hot nights on his cot in the army. Soon now, *soon*, he would see her again. And no one, not his arrogant, domineering mother nor his industrious brothers nor the bigoted Protestant clergy, would keep him from being with his little country sweetheart at last!

His family had despised him. Lazy, he was, they said. Mooning around with his head in the clouds instead of in the ledgers of the linen-woolen business of the family. Wasting time writing poetry about dreamy things. And then he became enamored of an Irish Catholic housemaid. That was the last straw. Perhaps the discipline of the army would change his attitude.

On that moonlit night before he was caught away, he had slipped an expensive golden ring on her slim finger, a symbol of their troth, and they promised each other to be faithful forever. She vowed to cherish it and the promise it bespoke as long as she lived. All he wanted was to take in his arms once more his lovely, sweet Mary.

Riding into town he came to the great stone walls

that surrounded Villa West, his family home. He remembered another time when he was at that very place. He had been coming home from a fair over in Ballinasloe, when he looked past a low-built wall of dry stone and saw, as in a misty dream, a girl beside the well in the meadow. In the bright sunlight she appeared to be lost in white glow. Two little ones played about her feet like sprites. To his idyllic eyes she was a vision, a faery image.

Then he recognized the sprites. They were the little girls of his sister, Maria. But he knew not the lovely young woman who hovered over them, laughing a light, breathless laugh.

William remembered that he dismounted and left his horse tied to the stile while he climbed over the rough stone wall and strolled across the grass toward the three girls. The glow faded somewhat as he neared the well. The young woman became less fairylike but more animated, with sparkling brown eyes and cheeks flushed rosy from the play.

"Well now," he said, coming closer to them. "Well, I recognize these little ones, but I don't believe I know you, lass?"

"It's Mary O'Connor, I am," she responded pleasantly. "My Da is a shoemaker down the lane, and I'm newly come to work in the grand house of Mulchinock."

Thinking about it now made him realize he had loved her from that moment on. When he walked with the girls to the house, when she served the family their dinner in the elaborate dining room that evening, when at the window he caught sight of her leaving the house in the twilight to go home, every moment of it was exciting to his soul.

His sister Maria, noticing how well the children got along with the kitchen maid, had made her their attendant. Their favorite play spot was in the meadow at the well, so Mary took them there almost daily. William Mulchinock made a habit of meeting them there. The little girls loved to have him come. He would sit on the grass next to the well with one of them on his knee and tell them stories of faeries and seal people and good old St. Patrick. Mary also would curl down nearby, thoroughly enjoying his tales while she busied her fingers mending the clothing of the little girls. Sometimes he put the stories in charming little rhymes, and the children would repeat them merrily. There was something sweet and gentle in his patient voice that seemed to touch Mary's heart.

To William, the wonder of her was her honesty. No silly flirtations, no putting on airs, she was Mary O'Connor, the daughter of a brogue-maker. Her mother was a no-nonsense O'Sullivan and a dairy maid at one of the big plantations. Mary adored her two younger sisters, Brigid and Ellen, and her little brother, Willie. She loved and respected her family and was proud of them. Her behavior was totally different from the giddy, pretentious girls of his class in Kerry.

William's mother felt differently. Margaret Mulchinock was the social leader of the community around Tralee. Since the death of her husband, Michael Mulchinock, she had kept a firm hand on the linen-woolen draper company and her sons.

"William Pembroke, I am beginning to be alarmed at your association with the kitchen maid," she said. "I don't know why you find her so attractive. Also, I have a feeling that she encourages you to fool around writing verses instead of getting your feet on the ground and learning the draper business."

"You must get to know her, Mother," William exclaimed. "She is quite sensible and does not ask favors. I'm afraid she does indeed encourage me to write. She understands that I am of a different sort than my brothers, more dramatic and literary. If Edward and Henry enjoy operating the business, then let them, but let me be myself."

"Be yourself? Does that include keeping company with a peasant girl? And a Catholic, at that? I have made every effort to keep her out of your sight when she is working here. Tell me, William, just how far has this gone? Is she loose? Should I have such a girl in my house? Does she have any hold over you?"

William's face flushed with anger at her accusation. "Nothing of that sort goes on. Believe it! She is a fine young woman. Decent. I won't have you say such things about her!"

Margaret looked at her son, defending a country girl, definitely not the kind that she wanted him to marry. Well then, let him play at romance. Young men liked to do things like that. But she would keep a close eye on the situation and if it became the least bit too serious, she would take whatever drastic steps necessary to control William's future.

William did not tell Mary of his mother's attitude. He loved the beautiful Irish lass and he was sure she loved him. Their times together were full of laughter and quiet talk and gentle understanding.

The cool shades of evening their mantle were
spreading
And Mary all smiling was listening to me.

Often they would stroll through the evening, finding beauty all around them, the black lace of trees against a huge horizon moon, the grace of ivy spilling over a stone wall. Sometimes he would lead her to the mossy stone bridge over a stream and they would sit quietly listening to the rush of crystal water below. As they walked through a narrow boreen, William would pluck a wild rose from a vine that offered them on outstretched leafy arms. He would present it to Mary as if it were a jewel, and she accepted it as such. He loved the curve of her soft cheek, the smoky shadows of her lashes as she gazed down at the delicate petals of the flower in her hands.

But, after his mother's remarks, he determined to flaunt his Mary and let Margaret try to explain it to her arrogant friends of the society in Tralee.

He stopped Mary in the pantry of the Mulchinock mansion one day and declared, "Mary, we are going to the dance at the crossroads tonight. I love lively music!"

"Oh, so do I," Mary exclaimed. "I would love to go!"

They went. The young people at the ceile, sons and daughters of tradesmen and farmers and brogue-makers, welcomed the wealthy William and pretty housemaid Mary with delight. The music of the pipes and fiddles and tin whistles filled the air. Thereafter, it became a weekly custom for the two of them to join in the jigs and reels and set dances, evenings of laughter and joyous, breathless exertion.

Then one evening William took Mary to sit on the stone bridge and watch the moonlight rippling with the wind across the water. The ocean breeze lifted her dark hair and let it fall across her rose-colored cheeks. William gently brushed it aside as he enclosed her shoulders with his arm and drew her to him.

"When I strayed with my love by the pure
crystal fountain,
That stands in the beautiful vale of Tralee"

"Mary O'Connor, do you know I love you?" he whispered.

Her dark, luminous eyes went wide with joy. "Oh, do you now, William Pembroke Mulchinock? And are you thinking I love you, too? Well then, you are right. I do love you, dear, gentle man."

A thrill of delight went through him. He held her more tightly and kissed her tenderly. Between them there was a mutual glow of happiness making them of one soul and mind.

Then he drew back from her a little. "Mary, you know I am the bad one in my family, the lazy dreamer who would rather layabout and write poetry than figure the profit from the sale of a length of Donegal tweed," he said.

"Ah, but there is need in the world for one the likes of you. Sure now, there is."

"I'm afraid my mother and brother don't see it that way. My younger brother, now he's a one who delights in the ledgers and merchandise. I am their eldest and their shame."

"Sad, it is. But they are your family. They have a right to want you to be a thriving gentleman."

"Do you believe I should settle down and become a good businessman?"

She looked at him, frowning with indecision. "Well now, I sure do not think that would be possible. You are a wonderful dreamer, William Pembroke. You have a beautiful soul. I'm afraid you would be a very bad businessman and, sure, you would stifle yourself and die if you had to cover it up and bury that which is in your heart."

Gently he leaned over and kissed her soft, pink lips. "Mary O'Connor, you understand me so well. Will you be kind to me and become my wife?"

Then Mary drew away. "I knew it would come to this," her voice broke with tears. "William Pembroke, I cannot marry you. Your family is wealthy and Protestant. I am poor and Catholic. Your mother and brother would never allow it. You would be cut off, penniless, outcast."

"Let them." He buried his face in her rich, dark hair. "I care not."

"And how would you live? Dreamers and poets do not make a good living. If we marry, soon we would become impoverished and hungry. Our children would starve. You would learn to hate me. No, no, William. We cannot marry. You must go away and meet someone else who your family will be pleased with."

Moonlight made silver streams of the tears that ran down her cheeks. He held her more tightly.

"Never! No one but you. Mary O'Connor, my Rose."

The next day, William told his mother that he had

asked Mary to marry him.

"And what did she answer?" Margaret asked.

"She said she would not. She had all sorts of good, sensible reasons why we should not. But she loves me. I will not accept her refusal. She is the dearest, most perfect girl in the world, and I know I can convince her. Accept that, Mother. You will learn to love her as I do."

Mrs. Mulchinock was silent, too silent. Her face was white. A strange glint came into her eyes. "I promise you will not marry her," she said at last in a voice like cold stone.

Fear washed over William like a shroud. That night he told Mary, "We must run away together, tonight. Mary, I fear for your safety!"

"Sure now, we cannot!"

There in the garden he held her close. "Mary, my little rose. I want . . ."

Her lips stopped his words. "I know what you want. So do I want to be with you forever, to marry you and have a home and little ones fathered by you. Oh, how much I want them! It cannot be. Go away, my grand love. Go to Dublin where your beautiful words will be found worthy. Let your soul be free. God has given you a gift far above the common, and it will be recognized some day. People will learn to love you as I do. Forget me, for the sake of your sweet soul. Someday you will write words that will be known and loved all over the whole wide world."

Slowly he slipped his hand in his pocket and drew out a tiny parcel wrapped in tissue paper.

"Mary, my rose, I will never marry anyone but you. I know you feel the same. This golden ring that I place on your finger is a token of my love for you. Give me your promise that you will keep it forever and never marry anyone but me. Someday, somehow we will find a way."

Mary looked at the simple shining circlet of gold with a large crystal stone set in it reflecting sparkling blue moonlight. It was pure and clean, a precious, fitting symbol of the sacred love they shared.

"Yes, William Pembroke Mulchinock, I promise with all my heart to wait for you as long as it must be."

The next morning as Mary washed the china breakfast dishes in the kitchen of the Mulchinock mansion, she heard a grand hubbub out in the street. People were chattering and calling out to one another. She hurried out the back door and ran around the garden in time to see William being escorted out through the front gate, obliged to mount up and ride down the street with a squad of British soldiers on horseback. Neighbors stood around commenting on the military uniforms. Mary stood still as stone. Where were they taking William? Would she ever see him again? A horrible sick feeling shot through her. On his horse, William looked back until his eyes found hers, his face white with despair. Lifting his hand, he silently bid her goodbye.

The cook of the house came up behind her. "It's conscription, is what it is. The English army is needing educated young men to serve as officers. Mary O'Connor, your fancy sweetheart is on his way to the Hell-hot India."

Mary's senses reeled. She was distracted and shaken all day, automatically going through the motions of her chores. It felt as if a heavy stone lay in her chest. Her mind was on that tender, young man being escorted away from his home and his love by a band of hardened soldiers. Then she was shaken wide awake with another blow.

Margaret Mulchinock sent for her to come to the drawing room.

"Mary O'Connor," she said with a satisfied tone, "I have taken steps to remove my son from your influence and your temptations. He has better things planned for him than poverty and marriage to one who dallies with young men in the night. Now I take steps to remove you from this family altogether. Certainly a stained woman like yourself is not fit to be associating with my little granddaughters. You will leave my employ and my house immediately. Nor will you be welcome to work for any other decent home in Tralee. I will see to it. Leave now and I hope never to see your face again! You are dismissed."

"Dismissed!" William was right. Something had happened, something dreadful. Mary was trembling, her face pale and white. Her reputation was destroyed, at least in Tralee and all plantations nearby. There was no way she could make it better. No one would believe her with Margaret Mulchinock's word against her own.

William was gone, gone to serve in the British army somewhere in the world. Would they break him? Would army discipline and reasonless obedience take away his gentle spirit and the wonderful words he wrote? She must pray to all the saints that would never happen!

She stumbled as she made her way through the boreen, her eyes were blinded by tears. It was indeed bad that she had lost her employment. The few pence that she earned had helped the family to have a bit of extra for clothing and tea and 'baccy for her Da. But it was worse, *much worse*, that her reputation was going to be talked about around the whole townland! She might never be able to earn money again in Tralee. She clutched her shawl to her shoulders, for it was autumn and the wind off the ocean was sharp. Winter was coming. The thought of the coming cold made her situation seem even more heartbreaking.

Oh, my William, my dearest love. I wish you were here now! Where have they taken you? Will your tenderness survive?

Mary was met at the door of the cottage by her red-haired younger sister, Brigid. The child was wild-eyed and frantic. Had she already heard of Mary's troubles?

"What is it, lass?" she asked.

"Oh, Mary, I'm so glad you're home already. It's the father! He was cutting a piece of leather for making brogues and the knife slipped. It's the most dreadful cut he has on his leg! I was going for Mam at the dairy house!"

"Don't go," Mary said, thinking that her mother must not trouble her employment now that Mary was not bringing in money. "Let me have a look first."

It was indeed the most dreadful gash angling across the top of his thigh! The blood poured and the flesh lay open. Her father sat on the floor, a stocky, gray-haired craftsman, leaning against the wall, staring at the unspeakable disaster that happened so quickly. How could this be? His face was gray, and weak chills set him to shaking. His worn trousers were already ripped away from the cut.

"There's no time for calling Mam! Brigid, get me the blanket off the cot. Hurry!" Mary shouted. She knelt down on the floor beside her Da, her skirts getting soaked in the blood there, and tore the old wool into strips. "Help me hold it together," she ordered Brigid.

The two girls worked to draw the flesh together and bind it in place. Then Mary ripped up her muslin petticoat to bandage the wound and try to stop the bleeding. It slowed but still ran.

"Thank the Blessed Virgin you came home early," thirteen–year-old Brigid said. "I didn't know what to do."

"I'm glad I did, too," Mary responded, but she could not tell her the reason. Ellen, eleven years old, and seven-year-old Willie sat in the corner clinging to each other and wailing at the terrible injury to their father. "Hush that howling!" Mary ordered. "Da must rest." Too much was happening too soon. Her dismissal from the mansion and now her father's dreadful injury! Inside herself, Mary was full of electric nerves that wanted to snap. She had to keep doing things, get control of her senses.

The Da was carefully stretched out on the floor now to keep his leg straight. He had gone unconscious, trembling all over. The girls covered him with an old fleece and a large apron and a tablecloth, every cloth they could find, to keep him warm.

Brigid went to bring her mother home. Mrs. O'Connor found her husband in the best condition he could be under the situation. His trembling had stopped, but he still looked gray and so weak. The tall, slim woman dropped to the floor and investigated the awful injury.

"You did well, my good girls," she said, pushing a stray graying hair from her forehead. "But we must try to keep it from becoming inflamed. You two, Ellen and Willie, do something to help your Da. Go out to the cow byre and gather cobwebs, lots of them, to pack his wound. Here, my fine husband." She raised him slightly, holding a cup of tea to his lips. "Drink some good stout tea. It will give you strength."

Mary stayed home with her father for several days while her mother continued to work at the dairy house. Finally then, her mother decided Mary could leave him for a while.

"I'm sorry about your job, child," Mrs. O'Connor told Mary. "Such things happen. And I grieve for you losing that fine young man, but you knew he was above you and him a Protestant heretic. Sure now, a marriage to him would never have worked. So then, it is time for the last haying of the season. Go and help the women pile up the cockeens in the fields. Brigid can take care of your Da now."

Mary looked at the tired face of her father as he lay on the cot by the fire. She was not sure he was getting better. In spite of the poultices of cobweb and potato, the cut on his leg was beginning to swell darkly and to redden angrily around the edges. But her mother said to go, and she did.

For two weeks he lay there, his family tending him the best they could. Gradually he became nauseous, then exhausted, then incoherent. Then he died.

Mary could not believe it. Not only had she lost the

man she desperately loved, until such time as he could come home, but now her dear father was gone. Why did it happen so? Her heart felt as if a terrible void hung there, empty from the loss of two dear ones. Her combined grief nearly tore her apart with anguished sobs.

Her mother allowed Mary and all the children to weep and wail at the wake. The neighbors helped with their keening and, sure Mrs. O'Connor let loose a torrent of tears, also. But, with her husband in the ground and his soul dutifully prayed for, she had to face life.

"Winter's coming, Mary," she said. "Without your Da's brogue-selling money, the few pence I earn will have to pay the taxes so we can keep our house. We're going to have to take great care burning the turf. He didn't have time to cut quite enough, and we've no money to buy it."

"I'm so sorry, Mam," Mary cried. "I never thought that the love of William Mulchinock would cost my family so dearly. I have tried to get a job, but Mrs. Mulchinock was true to her words. I am believed to be a scarlet woman. Not a house in Tralee will hire me."

"It's not your fault, Mary lass. I know you have done no wrong. William must be a grand fellow for you to love him so much."

"Grand, he is. And himself suffering right now in the misery of army life in a foreign land, only for the love of me. I'm cursed!"

"Not at all! Now, you will have to be the woman of the house while I work at the dairy. Mind the fires, keeping them low. Tend the bo, and milk her out good. We'll be needing the butter, too. Make the potatoes in the bin last the winter. Come the spring and you'll be cutting up the praties for the planting."

Mary did what she had to do. Never a long winter night went through but she wept for William and for her family. How could she have made it better? Should she have rebuffed William's company? Knowing quite well that his family would never approve of her, should she have pushed him away? Ah, but how could she, and him so gentle and lovely of soul.

And why did her father's hand slip that day after all the many, many pairs of brogues he had made with those strong fingers? Cursed, she was. It had to be. And she wondered if Margaret Mulchinock, Protestant that she was, did believe in curses and had brought one down on Mary.

As the winter days lengthened, she set herself beside the chimney every night and cut the seed potatoes into small chunks with an eye in each one. The warmer days finally came, when the hills were dug, and she dropped one piece in every hole along with a prayer. The children complained that she skimped on the potatoes at meals, and she admitted it, promising better helpings when the new potato harvest was brought in.

The harvest never came.

Bright green plants came up, promising fat little potatoes under the ground. Once or twice, Mary grubbled under the plants to search out the little brown marbles and see how they were doing. They were looking good. There would be a fine crop to fill the bin to overflowing for next winter's eating. She planted cabbages, too. Those things, along with some hearty loaves of soda bread with wheat flour bought from the landlord's mills, and the family would survive comfortably.

Then a terrible alarm sounded over the country! The potato vines were becoming sick overnight. They wilted. Black spots appeared on the leaves and they quickly shriveled away. Upon digging up the potatoes, all they found was stinking black slime! Not one good potato! The tenants had always depended on the potatoes from the little patches beside their huts to feed their families. Now there was nothing.

Oh, there were fields of corn and barley and wheat stretching out between the roads, and they were growing well. But that grain did not belong to the tenants. Tending those fields for the landlords paid the rent on their stone cottages often with only dirt floors. Fat cattle and herds of hogs were butchered and cured and shipped with the grain across the waters to be sold to profit the landlords.

But the peasant people had always survived on the butter and milk from one cow, an occasional small pig or chicken, *and the potatoes!*

The O'Connor family was caught with millions of other simple Irish folk without provisions for the next year. Mrs. O'Connor was forced to spend some of the pennies from her work at the landlord's dairy to buy bread for her children. At tax time, she did not have enough to pay, so the tax man took their cow. Without milk, the children became thin and weak. When the few cabbages were eaten and gone, Mary gathered wild greens and nettles to cook for her family.

Ellen and Willie wanted to set traps to catch a rabbit or perhaps go to the streams and catch fish. But that would be poaching on the landlord's property. It could mean the whipping post or even jail if they were caught.

Resistance to diseases went down. People fell ill from the most mild infections and died. Mrs. O'Connor gave her children the greater part of whatever bread she could get. She starved and became very weak. It was hard for her to lift and do her work at the dairy. Malnutrition sores broke out on her body. The land overseer saw those sores and fired her, lest she infect the landlord's produce.

Two years had passed since Mary had watched William Pembroke Mulchinock being escorted off to the army. From a time of joy in love and jolly times and well-fed good health, the O'Connors had come to starvation and despair. Mrs. O'Connor collapsed. It wasn't long before she and little Ellen died. Mary alone was left to provide for the thin, helpless children.

All the while, she had a secret. That wide golden ring, placed on her finger by William the night before he was lost to her, hung on a shoelace around her neck, close to her heart. Many times she wondered if she should sell it to buy food. How long would that food last before they were once more starving?

She was selfish, she knew, for the ring meant more to her than money. It meant hope, hope that someday soon things would change, that her loved ones would be fed and healthy again, hope that William would return to take her in his arms, to comfort her and all things would come right. Lying weak and sick on the slate floor of the dark, cold hut, her fingers caressed that small, shining token of beauty and love. Time and again that hope gave her strength to pull herself up and out of the cottage to search for something to feed the family.

She wanted to hate the people of Tralee. Mrs.

Mulchinock still lived in her grand house, and her sons rode their fine horses in the street and conducted a moderately prosperous business. Starving people often crawled the streets into town to beg, but they were driven out by the peelers to a workhouse where hundreds of people lay in the dirt outside the doors, arms outstretched for any scrap of food.

But she could not hate them. They could not know how awful were the horrors of hunger and deprivation. And sure, what could so few townspeople do to save the millions who were desperately hungry?

Brigid was now sixteen; Willie was twelve. All three of them wore rags that barely covered their pale, filthy, bony bodies. Surely it was only their youth that had kept them alive.

At last the day came when all hope was gone. They had, of course, been evicted from their cottage, for they could not pay the taxes and the landlord wanted to clear away all those hovels and expand his cattle herds. Mary and her brother and sister sat on the stone cliffs above Tralee Bay. They would die there, she knew. *Lie ourselves down and die and be done with it.*

She stared out of glassy eyes in her gaunt face at the ocean below. Her dark hair was thin and lank, her young hands blue between the white bones.

On the other side of that vast ocean was food. America had plenty of food. And jobs to earn the money to buy it. It was a land of plenty. So far away, unreachable. There was hope there.

Hope!

Quickly, Mary dragged her brother and sister to their feet.

"Come. Pull together all your strength. Brigid and Willie, you are going to America!"

The golden ring with the diamond set brought just enough. She bought food, just bread, so they could eat and gain some strength. A few old clothes to cover them decently were found and she filled a bag with bread to carry with them. Passage was bought on a boat leaving Tralee Bay for Queenstown where the children would take ship to America. The few pennies that were left, she tucked into Brigid's hand.

"What will you do?" Brigid wept.

"You are old enough to take charge and keep yourself and Willie safe on the trip," Mary scolded. "You are going to a beautiful land where there is food and the chance to live better than you ever will here. *I have given up the most precious thing in my life to give you this chance. Don't you fail!*"

She sat on the banks and watched the boat leave the harbor, the children lifting weak hands to wave goodbye to their homeland. Then she raised herself up and turned toward Tralee, trudging slowly across the stony meadows, to wait for her William to come back to her.

Now William rode along, coming home, wondering what he would find. Where would his Mary be now? She promised to wait for him, and he knew she would. He tried to spot her father's cottage but could only see several piles of rubble along the road where cottages used to be. Several thin, weary men carried a wooden coffin into a primitive burial ground becoming crowded with new graves.

"It's sorry I am to see so much misery and death in Tralee." William spoke to them sadly. "I've been gone these four years. I've missed many old friends. Who would that poor soul be that you're burying today?"

The leading carrier wagged his head sadly. "It's lucky you were to be gone from Ireland through these bad times," he answered. "As for this coffin, it carries a tragic tale, for it is a young woman who lost her love and now her life. It's Mary O'Connor."

Mary!

"Someday you will write words that will be known and loved all over the whole wide world," quoth Mary.

❧

And so he did. On a marble stone under a cross outside Tralee the words are written:

> *"She was lovely and fair as the Rose of the Summer,*
> *Was Mary, The Rose of Tralee."*

Speranza, Lady Wilde

The Nation, *that was the name of the rebel newspaper distributed by the Young Irelanders in the mid 1800s. That aggravating yen to be free of British rule popped out again, this time in print. Stories, articles, and poems saturated its pages with unrest, outrage, and Irish patriotism. Generally, the works were not signed, except with blind pseudonyms. Most of the features presented to the Irish people the unbelievably unfair, heartless realities of the Famine and British rule. The English courts called the publishers of* The Nation *traitors.*

Jane Francesca, I forbid you to go to the offices of that seditious newspaper! I will not have you associating with that crowd of revolutionaries. How will it look, the daughter of an archdeacon of the Church of Ireland joining herself with the Young Irelanders and contributing inflammatory words to a newspaper that is clearly made up of traitors?"

"Traitors to whom?" the girl spoke back. "Traitors to the Crown of England or traitors to our own Irish blood? The real traitors in Ireland are the Ascendancy snobs who stole our lands and now let our people die in the roads of starvation. Look around you, Father. Have pity on those poor country people."

"The Famine in the land is not our concern. Living here in Dublin, we are not a part of that problem. Now, I forbid you—"

"Father dear, you refuse to see that which is under your nose. The poor who are evicted from their little farms have no place to go but Dublin. If they don't die of starvation in the countryside, they must crowd into Dublin tenements and die of filth and disease. Ask the doctor who stands there behind you. He surely knows the facts."

"Jane, I forbid you—"

It was too late to say it again. Jane had her bonnet strings tied under her pretty, round chin, leaving only dark curls clustered beside her cheeks. One more flash of zealous brown eyes and she tossed her shawl about her shoulders. Her bouffant skirts swished out the door before he could finish his declaration.

Archdeacon Elgee was sitting on a settee near the fireplace in the vicarage. He laid his head against the back of the settee again after Jane popped out the door. Standing behind the little couch, the doctor leaned over the minister's head and proceeded to wash out his eyes with a tiny cup of warm salt water.

"What am I to do, Dr. Wilde?" the minister moaned. "My daughter is a headstrong thorn in my side. She could be arrested. *She could be hanged!* Stubborn. Disobedient. How can I control her?"

The doctor, a man in his thirties, with unkempt, sand-colored hair and a tacky, faded frock coat, continued his treatment of the tired, red eyes of the minister while he thoughtfully responded, "She has an amazing ability to put words to paper. I believe she is talented that way."

"You read *The Nation* newspaper? I mean . . ." he stammered, "where have you read her writings?"

Dr. William Wilde quietly wiped the potion away from the eyes of his patient. "Everyone reads it, sir. Charles Gavan Duffy and that group are making some poignant arguments for more freedom for the Irish. 'Speranza' is one of my favorite contributors to the publication."

Elgee blinked his eyes open in alarm. "Have you known that Speranza is my daughter? Does everyone in Dublin know?"

"Have no fear, sir. As a physician, I have taken an oath never to disclose anything I hear while treating a patient. She has an amazing ability to express the conditions of the poor in Ireland. Her poem "The Famine Years" brought me to tears. If you fear for her well-being, you might consider finding her a good husband to keep her too busy with children and home to have time to make trouble with her patriotic views."

Elgee sighed with relief and despair. "But what man will want such a one for a wife? A woman should be small and demure, gentle and shy. She is too tall, too sturdily built, and surely too outspoken."

"She has her own interesting personality, sir," the

doctor said quietly as he packed up his medicine bag to take his leave.

"Interesting indeed. I tremble to think she might marry one of those radicals."

It was late that night when Jane opened the outer door of a dank and dirty office in the neighborhood south of the River Liffey. She could see the dark outline of the spire of St. Patrick's cathedral beyond the tall, ugly tenement buildings around her, and she wished she were closer to that sanctuary instead of stepping out into the black night alone on the shadowy street. Taking her kerchief out of her reticule, she held it over her nose in a futile attempt to obscure the fetid smells of grimy pools and human waste on the cobblestones.

As quietly as she could, she closed the door behind her and began to slip down the street as close to the buildings as her hooped skirts allowed, hoping and fervently praying that no one would see her. Her efforts to be invisible were fruitless. From doorways and corners dark figures began to move.

At first she walked in desperate fear and dread. Here she was, a girl alone in the dark night in the Liberties, the worst crime and poverty-ridden part of the city. Horrible stories came back to her of clergy and police who had business there being murdered and hung up on posts. What would they do to a young lady? It was too awful to imagine!

Then she became angry. How dare they threaten her? She was down there in the swill and pestilence because of their poverty! Her work was to try to make life better for these people. If anyone came close to reaching for her, she would pound him into the road. Let

them try! She clutched the heavy package of newspaper materials and braced herself.

Suddenly she heard the rattle of carriage wheels behind her and she turned. The lone driver pulled up beside her.

"Young lady, who are you and what are you doing here in the Liberties, and at this time of night? Get yourself into this buggy immediately!" came a muffled voice.

Someone called gruffly out of the shadows, "Is that you, Doc? Is she your woman? Better get her on out of here!"

"I will indeed, Matt. See to it that we make it to the cathedral without any trouble, will you, lad?"

"That I will," the voice answered, with a clear challenge to all who would interfere. The dark figures melted back into the walls and doorways.

The driver reached and grabbed Jane's hand, yanking her up into the vehicle, almost causing her to drop her package. Then he slapped the reins on the shabby, old horse, and the carriage rolled forward with a jerk.

"Now then," said the man beside her. "Are you mad, walking alone in this part of Dublin, and in the dark night, at that?"

"I am not mad!" Jane retorted. "I have good reason to be here. If those people only knew, I am working for them."

"And how would that be?"

"Are you familiar with the newspaper *The Nation*?"

"I am." There was surprise in his voice.

"Well then, I came here to deliver a verse to be printed in this week's issue, and I found that the editor has been arrested for sedition. Without Charles Gavan Duffy, they were having a bad time finishing it. I had to stay and help get it ready for the press. But my father will be expecting me home tonight. He is likely already livid because I am so late. The men at the office tried to get me to wait until daylight or at least until I had an escort, but I had to go."

"*The Nation* is prepared here in the Liberties?" the man asked, curious.

"So it is, but don't be getting ideas about turning us in to the peelers." Jane looked sharply at the man. He wore a large, black hat low over his face and a muffler wrapped almost to his eyes. In the dark, she could see no features. "We can move the offices so quickly that they cannot be followed."

"You need have no worry about that," he said.

They rode through the gloom of the slum streets silently heading for the big, old church. Jane looked around and spied something behind them in the floor of the rickety vehicle.

"What is that?" she said and, before the driver could stop her, she pulled aside a musty, heavy cloth to see.

"A body!" she screamed. "You have a dead body back there. Who are you? What are you? A ghoul! A murderer? Let me off this buggy right now!"

She started to jump out of the moving carriage, but he caught her. "You can't go yet. It's not safe. Stay here!"

"I will not!" Jane doubled her fingers into a fist and struck the man's head, knocking his muffler away from his face and his hat aside, revealing rumpled hair. Dim light fell on his features.

"Dr. Wilde! It is you! What are you doing here, and with a dead body?" Jane sat still on the carriage seat, stunned.

"Now, Miss Elgee, if you will listen I will try to explain, but don't be appalled. I accepted your explanation for being in this Godforsaken place, now you listen to mine. And don't hit me again. That hurt!"

With quiet resignation, the doctor told her about his work. "How can one study the human body without a body to study?" he reasoned. "I am interested in phrenology. You don't understand? Phrenology is the hypothesis that the shape of a human skull will give evidence of that person's personality, whether he has criminal tendencies or he is a scholar."

In spite of herself, Jane was intrigued. "What an interesting idea," she said. "But, what are you doing with this body?"

"The only place to appropriate a cadaver is a graveyard or the place where human life is cheap and a dead body is a marketable commodity. Digging respectable people out of their graves is frowned upon. Therefore, I must purchase a body where the few pence paid means life or starvation to the seller."

"How terribly sad," Jane said. "Very well, I understand. I'm sure it is against the law."

"Just so as it is against the law to publish revolutionary newspapers."

"Shall we then make a pact?"

"If you are willing."

"I am."

That settled, the doctor tossed the cover again over his property, and they moved on. He drove her all the way across the city in the dark night, over a bridge crossing the Liffey, and through spotless Georgian house fronts to a crossroad street very near the vicarage. As he helped her down off the carriage, he spoke politely.

"Have a good evening, Miss Elgee. I encourage you to keep writing. You have an amazing talent."

"I'm afraid I cannot return the compliment about your avocation, Dr. Wilde. Thank you for your kind assistance."

There was quite a stir among the Young Irelanders and all of Dublin when the news came out about Duffy's arrest. The people, Irish and English, rich and poor, all over Ireland, had been captivated by *The Nation.* After much time in Dublin Castle's prison ward, Duffy was brought to trial. The gallery of the court building was filled with spectators. The British lawyers in their stern white wigs were quite certain they had reason to dispose of Duffy either on a gallows or a slave ship and, in so doing, would put a stop to the inflammatory newspaper.

On the front line of the gallery, Jane Francesca Elgee sat, neatly gloved hands resting on the rail. Her dark hair was clustered in curls tucked inside a proper straw bonnet, but it lacked the many bows and flowers that were so popular among prim young ladies of the day. Her shawl was draped over a simple broadcloth suit of daring Irish green, and her wide brown eyes were intent on the proceedings down below.

Charles Gavan Duffy stood in the dock, accused of inciting rebellion against the Crown. A row of robed judges sat at the bench, casually watching the proceedings before them, undoubtedly certain that conviction was a given. The prosecutor adjusted his wig and stood forth. He lambasted Duffy for the traitorous words in his publication.

Jane became more and more angry as his dissertation went on. *The Nation* was merely printing the truth about unspeakable suffering of the Irish people at the hands of the English rulers. The prosecutor never spoke about the dreadful conditions of the poor farmers who were beaten down, treated like slaves, dying from hunger and cold, thrown out of their hovels by the so-called Ascendancy landlords. Her softly rounded body stiffened, and it was plain that she wanted terribly to interrupt and defend the reasons for the printing of the newspaper.

Then the white-wigged accuser read quotes from the paper, some written by Duffy, some by Thomas Davis, another editor of the audacious press. Many written by anonymous persons with names such as "Mary" or "John" or "*Speranza*."

What if someone who knew the identity of "Speranza" spoke up and named her also as a seditionist? Her father's fears would be fulfilled. She would surely hang.

Somehow the thought made no difference to Jane. At this point, she was too completely filled with fury at the injustice of calling the Young Irelanders "traitors." Especially insulting was naming Charles Gavan Duffy who was noble and only pointed out the truth when he printed those pages.

Finally the lawyer raised a newspaper in his hand and shouted, "If all of the words I have read to you before have not convinced this court that this man, Charles Gavan Duffy, should be convicted of inciting to treason, this will certainly prove his guilt!"

He read aloud:

"We must bring forth in Ireland one hundred thousand muskets, we must charge forth to battle for the long pending war with England has already commenced."

Then he called out to the judges, "Gentlemen, have you ever heard more treasonable, more flagrant provocation to insurrection in your life? And written by the hand of the prisoner, Duffy, who stands here before you!"

That did it! Jane was on her feet. All eyes turned to see the tall, young woman who rose from her seat and stood boldly at the rail. She did not beg permission to speak. She did not apologize for interrupting the proceedings. Her voice was sharp and clear and rang out in the vaulted hall.

"I, and I alone, am the culprit, if culprit there be! I wrote that editorial!"

Silence. The prosecutor was stunned. The judges looked at each other, not sure what to do. Here was a young woman announcing to the court that she was guilty of writing a blatantly treasonable statement. Should she be arrested? The murmur of approval for her boldness that came from the gallery made them choose to do otherwise.

They stammered about and finally decided to ignore the incident. However, the power of the prosecutor's case was diluted. His words lacked emphasis. He was prepared to convict a nuisance of a man, a perpetrator of traitorous writings. The lawyer had been ready to sentence a man to the horrors of prison in an English jail or slavery or to be hung by the neck until dead, when a bold young lady had pulled his case from under him. Instead, the court was confounded by the open confession of the girl.

Jane sat down, crossed her arms, and silently dared them to arrest her before the crowd that day. Every day thereafter, she was there, and so she remained until the trial ended.

She was unaware that, in a far back corner of the gallery, Dr. William Wilde had watched her spirited confession with a certain gleam of amusement and pride in his eyes.

The case against Duffy staggered and fell flat. Days later he was set free and went right back to his work, publishing The Nation.

It would seem that Archdeacon Elgee had a great deal of trouble with his eyes, for the doctor visited his home often, sometimes without pay. Elgee was flattered and pleased to have him come, after all the doctor had, over years, gained great respect in Ireland and England for his study of ocular problems and finding their solutions. Dr. Wilde explained to the archdeacon that his was an unusual case that he wanted to investigate carefully.

Somehow, Jane was always home when he came. They said little to each other, only a casual glance or courteous word now and then.

"What are you writing these days now that *The Nation* is discontinued?" the tattered doctor asked her on one occasion.

"I have been preparing to translate some of the classic literature of Europe, and I am making a study of Irish folklore," she answered. "After so many centuries without any physicians to heal their wounds and illnesses, the farmers have had to come up with their own healing. It is a mixture of ancient Druid potions and rites and experimentation with herbs, both added to their simple faith in their religion. It's a fascinating subject. I plan to write a book on it."

"Write a book?" her father mimicked sarcastically. "Wasting your time writing poetry and foolish books. Why are you not being courted? You need to get married! You need to be raising children and doing something worthwhile. I'll not be around forever, Jane Francesca, and you will need a husband. You're not getting any younger."

A small smile tugged at the doctor's lips at the lecture, while he continued his ministrations to the archdeacon's eyes.

"Please pardon me for disagreeing, sir," he said. "But I believe your daughter has fine writing talent and she will do well for herself."

The minister muttered a few words of argument, but he did not carry it further just then. He didn't want to annoy the grand physician from whom he received free treatments. He had plenty of time to continue ranting at his daughter when the doctor was not there.

Most of Jane's research was done out in the hinterlands, questioning farmers and their wives. Now that the Famine was easing up, those people who were left were very willing to welcome her into their cottages and share their primitive knowledge. She also enjoyed perusing the wonderful collection of books at Trinity College Library.

One sunny day as she crossed the inner square of

the campus, she passed a gathering of young male students in their short coats and tall, black silk hats, lounging at the door to the examination hall. She overheard one of the fellows say, "There he is now, old Willie Wilde, going into the library. It's a wonder they allow him in there. He might touch some fine books and they would disintegrate. He has outlandish ideas and his old clothes are so grimy. Surely he hasn't cut or combed his hair in years. Have you ever noticed his hands? I'll bet he digs in the cemeteries at night to find the bodies of convicts so he can examine the lumps on their heads. How else could anyone get his fingernails so dirty?"

"Why, his nails get dirty from scratching *his* body." another boy answered, and the whole group laughed hysterically.

They did not notice the tall, attractive young woman whose path made a sharp turn to come toward them. Suddenly she was there, towering over them, her brown eyes almost red with fury.

"How dare you speak that way about that fine doctor!" she demanded. "He is brilliant. His knowledge of ocular problems will soon earn him knighthood from Queen Victoria. You are so busy primping yourselves to look like a bunch of dandies that you don't even know the finest quality professional when you see him. Not one of you will ever reach his greatness, you are so filled with conceit and silly-headedness. Ignorant jackasses, the lot of you!"

Jane stalked off, leaving the students flabbergasted. Her bonnet had dropped back during her tirade, her rich dark hair was disheveled, but she walked like a queen, her full skirts flouncing at every outraged step.

"Who was that?"

"*What* was that?"

"Was she right? Is old, dirty Willie Wilde going to be knighted?"

"Wait until this gets around!"

It got around. Even old, dirty Willie heard about it. It was true that he had received notice that the queen of England was going to honor him for his work in ocular science, never mind his curiosity about phrenology.

Jane had defended him. What a great lady she was! They had been friends at a distance for a long time, ever since that night in the Liberties. He shuddered to think what would have happened to the girl if he had not chanced to be there. But he *was* there, and a mutual if silent respect had grown between them.

One evening when the archdeacon was attending a theological conference, William Wilde appeared on the vicarage doorstep. The housemaid let him in when he said he had not come to attend to Mr. Elgee's eye problems but to see his daughter.

Jane greeted him with curiosity and seated him opposite her on the other settee before the fire.

"I have a very particular reason for this visit, Miss Elgee," he said, watching her smooth, round face, the way her soft, dimpled hands caught the light from the fire, the glow of satin stretched tightly over her full bosom.

"Have you then?" Jane's dark brown eyes expressed interest, and she waited for the likeable gentleman to continue, intrigued.

"I don't believe you are walking out with anyone, are you?"

Jane's eyes grew embarrassed as she admitted that, at the advanced age of twenty-five, she had no suitors.

Dr. William Wilde, his hair slightly combed, hands fairly clean, still wearing the battered frock coat, which likely was the only one he bothered to own, leaned forward and spoke. "You have a way with letters and words, Miss Elgee. I know only how to say what I came to say and do it plainly."

Jane was stunned. What in the world was the doctor trying to say with such deliberate words? Was something dreadfully wrong with her father? Had some political factor lost Dr. Wilde his knighthood? *Say it, man, and get on with it!*

"Jane Francesca Elgee, I have watched you for several years now, ever since we met in the Liberties. I believe you are of a special nature like myself, an 'eccentric' if you will. Not the same, of course. You are fastidious and elegant about your person and fashions. I care nothing about such things, except as required by the laws of decency.

"You are an exciting, fascinating woman. I admire your boldness and your dedication to freedom. I stand in awe of your brilliance with literature and poetry. You are a person to hold in high regard.

"As for me, I pour my whole self into my work and my avocation. I know the students at the college make fun of me. I have a reputation for ghoulish tendencies that makes people withdraw from my company. I care not. I have no time for social life.

"We are a pair of nonconformists. I admire you for your independence. I have heard that you expressed some respect for me, as I am. I hope that is true."

"It is true. I do indeed have respect for you."

"Thank you, lady. Now then, I have developed some public notice for my work in ocular care and treatment. I have been told that I am soon to be knighted for this. For that reason, I am able to offer a comfortable living to a wife. Jane, Miss Elgee, I could not bear a conventional wife, a sweet little brainless thing who will produce many babies and drive me insane with constant chatter about the price of cabbage and little Toby's teething. I do not want to hear harangues about my toilette or lack of it.

"I want a real woman whom I can respect for her own accomplishments. I want a woman I can be proud of in her own right, with whom I can share a home and a child or two and go about my occupations without hindrance.

"My wife would have her own life, also. You could draw around you intellectual, stimulating people and compare notes on literature and politics, in which I know you delight.

"Jane Francesca Elgee, will you share your life with me as two unique beings in a world filled with dull gray porridge? Speranza, will you become Lady Wilde?"

Her dark brown eyes shone with new affection for the man she had known for so long, who clearly knew her well, and cared for the lovely woman she was. Sometime past, she had accepted the belief that she would never appeal to any gentleman as a wife. Jane Francesca Elgee was a whole person in herself and too outspoken, too engrossed in her pursuit of knowledge, too tall and strong-minded to be submissive to the will of the customary head of the house figure.

Now here was a fine man, honored in his profession, intrigued by the curious ways of nature, a man she also respected and admired for the person he was, offering her affection and the kind of wonderful life perfect for her. And he *wanted* her!

Her heart warmed and thrilled as she said, "William Wilde, I will."

They married. The public said they deserved each other. Sir William Wilde continued his research. Lady Wilde wrote her books, which became basic educational tools in Ireland. She held soirees in their apartments in Dublin and surrounded herself and their little son with the world of artists and poets, musicians and dramatists. Theirs was a good life.

∽൭∾

Speranza died in 1896, well respected for her literary works and her powerful stand on freedom in Ireland.

Oh, yes, their son was named Oscar Fingal O'Flahertie Wills Wilde. They called him Oscar Wilde.

Kitty O'Shea and the Uncrowned King

Parnell. *The name struck a chord of hope in the hearts of Irishmen everywhere. Charles Stewart Parnell, a Protestant landlord had gotten himself elected to the united English-Irish Parliament in the second half of the 1800s. He was holding fast to his goal of separating the governing bodies, allowing Ireland to have its own "Home Rule." Tall, handsome, and daring, he cleverly negotiated proper procedures in the Parliament designed to bring about the long hoped-for legislation. To the Irish, he was the Uncrowned King. Even the British admired him . . . to an extent.*

Kitty, my love, come with me. I want you to meet someone."

Captain William O'Shea slipped his hand under the white-gloved arm of his pretty wife and tugged.

She held back. "Oh, Willie, please don't make me

meet another of those dreadful politicians. I get so bored! And please remember that I don't like to be called 'Kitty.'"

"All right, Katharine, but those politicians don't find *you* boring. Your little flirts thrill their stuffy, old souls and make them think twice about me when I sit in the House of Commons. Now, come. The fellow I am going to introduce to you isn't old. Twenty-eight years, I believe. He is the MP who sponsored me in the County Clare election that brought us here to London. Do you remember the great Charles Stewart Parnell?"

"Yes, I remember," Katharine nodded. "Very well, I will try to be nice to him. But believe this, Willie O'Shea, I know what you are doing. You have not been a true husband to me since the day we were married. We don't even live together. You would rather dally with my silly sister. You only use me to attract attention to yourself."

William propelled her through the party crowd of people in the German Embassy. The music of a string ensemble and the prattle of jolly conversation covered his next words, which he uttered in a low, threatening voice.

"Listen to me, Katharine O'Shea, you will do as I tell you. I provide you with a comfortable flat and everything you need. As far as my attentions go, I will choose when and how I see you and for what purpose. Now then," his voice rose quickly to a cheerful pitch. "Mr. Parnell, may I introduce my dear wife, Katharine? She has been frantic to meet you."

Katharine gave her husband a look of irritated frustration before turning toward the gentleman.

The tall man with a well-trimmed dark beard and intense brown eyes took her gloved hand and bowed courteously over her fingers.

"I am flattered, madam," he said. "And greatly pleased to meet such a lovely lady."

Katharine curtsied smoothly, her pale green satin skirt and bustle swaying slightly with her movement. This one didn't look as bad as the other Members of Parliament. He was quite handsome, and his black frock coat and slim trousers fit neatly on his lean frame. She reached up and tucked away a stray curl in her full auburn hair, and her blue eyes brightened with interest.

Willie spoke up, "Charles, you must lead my treasure out to dance. You will find her quite accomplished."

"To be sure." Parnell led the lady along the wall of the crowded room to an arched doorway that opened into a larger ballroom. The string ensemble played an enticing waltz.

As they danced he said very little. Try as he would to glance occasionally around the room at the beruffled ladies and the gentlemen elegant in black, he could not take his eyes off his dance partner. She was such a pretty little thing dressed in grand fashion, her gown cut low in front, her figure packed neatly into a perfect S-shape, with narrow waist and pleated skirt and bustle.

Katharine's blue eyes were merry, recognizing his fascination with her and liking it. So many of those MPs were old, with noses red from too much porter, and they were stout, ungainly dancers. Parnell's steps were smooth and accurate. The two moved in pleasant accord across the dance floor.

"Mr. Parnell, where did you learn to dance so well?"

she inquired.

He smiled stiffly, as if a smile was not his customary expression. "I have two sisters, madam. They would not turn me loose on the world without proper training. I shall take care to let them know you approve of their efforts."

From the side of the archway, Captain O'Shea watched, pleased with his manipulations. Parnell had been helpful to him in supporting his election campaign, but there were plenty of future times coming when O'Shea could find his backing useful. Kitty's charm might bring the great man further into his camp.

"He will owe me!" William felt a thrill of developing power. It was a clever move, marrying Katharine Woods. Her sister was indeed more vivacious and satisfying, but Katharine was captivating. She could charm those lords and MPs, making them aware of him, until William could work his way into their confidence. Besides, it was not Katharine's sister who was their Aunt Ben's favorite, who would soon be inheriting the old woman's fortune. Mrs. Benjamin Woods was close to ninety years old and very wealthy and, more than once, had expressed her wish that darling Katharine would receive all that she had upon her death. O'Shea ran a salacious tongue across his lips at the thought, smoothed the lapels on his coat, and patted his curly, blonde hair carefully into place.

He was quite handsome, you know, with his blonde mustache and his military bearing. The ladies smiled at him, and his flattery sent them into spasms of giggles. But it wasn't the ladies he needed to impress. Katharine's attraction to the gentlemen glided smoothly over to himself.

One more glance at the pair on the dance floor and he left the doorway to mingle with his contemporaries.

The waltz ended. Parnell loosed his touch on Katharine's waist and hand. Looking down at her he asked, "Would Madam like to have some refreshments? I will gladly bring you something."

"Please call me Katharine," she said. "I hope we are going to be friends. Truly, I wish no sweets or drink. I believe the air in the garden would be more refreshing. It's rather close and warm in here."

"Certainly. As you wish." He took her elbow and steered her toward the wide-open French doors.

The garden paths were faintly lighted by paper-covered candles. Katharine could see other couples strolling along the walkways, sitting on stone benches beside large flowering shrubs, and standing close together beneath decorative trees in the dark. Parnell found an unoccupied bench and she sat down, fanning herself from the exertion of the waltz.

As soon as her escort had made himself comfortable at the other end of the bench she asked, "So you have two sisters? Where do they live? In Ireland, I'm sure."

"They do live in Ireland, at our family home, Avondale, in Wicklow."

"Then you are a landlord?"

"Indeed, a Protestant and a land owner, but I prefer not to think of myself as a 'lord.' Those farmers who work on our lands deserve to be free from being 'lorded' over."

"You have sympathy for the tenant farmers, then?"

"I do. That is my purpose in being here in the Irish

delegation to the House of Commons. I intend to do everything in my power to bring Home Rule to our country so that those farmers can own the land they work and every Irishman, Protestant or Catholic, will have some control over those who lead them. With Ireland's own Parliament, their votes will have greater effect."

A new respect shone in Katharine's eyes. "I admire your goal, sir."

The man gazed for a while at the sincere young woman beside him. She was not giddy or silly. It was clear that she meant what she said.

"Please call me Charles," he said. "I believe we *are* going to be friends."

"Then tell me more. Tell me how you came to believe in this freedom."

"I believe much of my attitude comes from my mother. She was born in America. Her parents were Irish, and fought in the American Revolution. She finds the plight of the tenants outrageous in Ireland, and she is not afraid to say it. It is appalling that human beings must live on mud floors in raw stone huts. My father agrees. As for my sisters, Fanny and Anna, if ever there were two militant soldiers for helping the poor, they are those. And they are not foolish. Fanny writes rebellious poetry, and both of them work in the Land League, putting pressure on the landlords to give their farmers a decent living."

"Such fine people, your family. Charles, I should like to meet them someday."

He smiled just a little. "Perhaps someday you may."

Suddenly a voice spoke behind them. "Well now, I

believe the two of you are getting along fine!" William said. "I wish we could stay longer and I could join your conversation, but I must be getting Katharine home. The night air isn't good for her, you know."

Parnell rose to his feet and extended his hand to help Katharine rise. "It has been a pleasure visiting with you, madam," he said.

"Why, Charles old boy, if you enjoy the company of my wife, feel free to call on her at home. You are welcome to do so." *And I shall drain her of every word he says and use it to my advantage,* William told himself.

Parnell's dark eyes grew wider at the blatant invitation to call on Mrs. O'Shea by himself. Katharine frowned with fury at Will's offer. It cheapened her.

However, it was a few days later that the doorbell rang at Katharine's flat in Eltham. A quiet voice asked Peg, the maid, to give his card to Mrs. O'Shea and see if she was "at home" to company. When Peg brought the card to Katharine, the lady was far from ready to accept callers. She sat reading in her bedroom, wearing her dressing gown. But one look at the card and she jumped to her feet.

"Seat him in the parlor, Peg. Get him tea. Don't let him leave. I'll be ready to see him in two shakes of a lamb's tail! Go! Take care of him until I get there!"

With amazing speed, she yanked off the robe, squirmed into her corset and petticoats, and pulled on a gown of crisp, blue linen. Drawing her auburn hair away from her face, she fastened it high on the back of her head with a wide bow. She patted a touch of talc on her face and hurried through the hall and into the parlor, cheeks flushed and eyes bright.

Charles Stewart Parnell appeared rather flustered at her welcome. He wasn't sure he should be there, after all. Katharine was a bit confused as to the purpose of his call, but she was truly delighted to see him and she could not help but show it.

It was such a pleasant visit. They shared small sandwiches and tea cakes. They talked about their respective homesteads and families. Katharine told him about her dear Aunt Ben. Charles told her about his friend, Michael Davitt, the fine little man who had lost his arm as a child laborer in a Lancashire linen factory, and now was the brains behind the Land League, and no doubt was connected with the Fenians, who were tormenting unreasonable landlords.

Katharine did her best to encourage Charles in his determination to get Home Rule for the Irish, a Parliament of their own. It pleased him to hear her response.

Before they knew it, two hours had passed. He rose and Katharine sent Peg for his hat and cane.

"I cannot tell you how much I have enjoyed our conversation," Katharine told him at the door.

"As have I, Katharine," he said. "It rather helps me to air my views so that I get a better perspective before I need to present them to the Powers That Be. I hope I have not taken up too much of your time."

"Not at all. Please call again, Charles."

He did. Several times more. Each time they found a greater kinship in their policies on civic matters, their hopes for the future, their ideals.

And each time they parted, it was with more regret, more gentle reluctance. When Charles took her hand in parting he held it longer, their eyes speaking the words they dared not say aloud. It was there—a tender yearning to be more than just friends, to touch one another with caresses that would make them closer, blending their two persons to become one.

It was too late. Katharine was tightly married to a greedy, contriving man. He would never give up his control and uses for her. Charles was honorable. He should not even be unwillingly coveting another man's wife, even though Katharine had made it clear that it was a marriage in name only.

At last, leaving her at her door, he took a deep, shaky breath and said it. "This is the last time I will have the pleasure of your company, Mrs. Katharine O'Shea. I'm sure you know my feelings. I cannot bear to be near you like this, becoming more and more in love with you, knowing that I have not a chance to fulfill the foolish hopes in my heart. I will not come again."

Tears poured from her eyes. Katharine looked up into that handsome face, that dear person whom she also had learned to love. She wept without shame. He wanted to take her in his arms and comfort her, but he dared not and she knew it. The door closed between their love, and it was over.

The next time they saw each other was at a gathering to honor Queen Victoria's birthday. Invitations had been sent out, and anyone who did not appear had better be at death's door. Katharine had been in a state of depression for two months and did not want to go. She didn't tell William that she was sure Charles Stewart Parnell would be there and she did not want to see him. She told him she was ill.

"You will go!" he stated. "You are not ill, only spoiled. I haven't required you to make an appearance for weeks. This is the most important event of the season. Every MP and his wife must be there, and you will be."

She went. She deliberately wore a stunning *black* gown. The floating folds of organza gave her a look of mystery but also mourning. When William came for her, he was angry at the color but there was no time to change.

The crowd in the ballroom was immense. Perhaps, in such a throng, neither Charles Parnell nor Katharine would spy the other. But they did.

In fact, William was busily making contact with every important personage he could find and introducing his beautiful wife to all who had not had the pleasure before, even Prime Minister William Gladstone. And there was Parnell.

"Charles, my good fellow," William called across the refreshment tables. "Come over here. Here is my Katharine. I understand the two of you have become great friends, having an occasional tea together and discussing politics. I'm glad. Never can seem to get her interested in those things. Kitty love, stay here with Parnell while I catch up with the Prince of Wales. If I can, I will be back to fetch you."

Alone. Hundreds if not thousands of people milled about around them, but they were alone. Katharine O'Shea and Charles Stewart Parnell.

Their eyes met. It was hopeless. Powerful emotion welled up and overcame all their noble resolutions. They were engulfed in the greatest love. Waves of tenderness washed over them while they stood there, delicious, wonderful, amazing, overpowering joy!

"Tomorrow," he said.

"Tomorrow."

"I met him!" William came back. "He shook my hand. I wanted him to meet you, Kitty, but he is surrounded. Next time I will be sure he does. Kitty, Katharine, you are trembling. What is wrong?"

"I told you I was not well, Willie. You must take me home."

"Soon. As soon as I can, but there are so many people I want to meet my beautiful wife. Come now, you will be all right. It's just the excitement. Goodbye, Charles. See you in the Chambers." He took her arm and dragged her off into the crowd.

Parnell frowned, wondering if she really was ill and if Willie O'Shea never gave her any better concern than that when she was not well.

And so it was. The next afternoon, the great man knocked on the door of the flat in Eltham. The maid let him in. In the evening, Peg went home. Charles did not.

Very quietly and with total joy they lived together. Charles, of course, kept his residence in London during the sessions of Parliament. But their life was shared in Katharine's home.

William found out about it. It was no particular secret. They only did what they could to keep it quiet, and Charles' acquaintances chose to overlook it, in spite of the fact that it was carried on in prudish Victorian England and with the knowledge of many in morally inflexible Catholic Ireland.

At first William told himself that he *must be outraged,* after all she was his wife! But then he realized he really didn't care. He didn't bother to take her to social events any more. If a fat old MP claimed he missed her, William simply pled her ill health. And William went to his own quarters and slept with the lively sister of Katharine, all the time keeping a firm grip on his wedding papers to the heiress to Aunt Ben's money.

Charles Parnell was not often "home" with his love. First there was a trip to America to help the wonderful Clan na Gael raise money to support the Land League. He made some rather inflammatory speeches in New York and Cincinnati. When he came home to Ireland, Prime Minister Gladstone was dealing with boycotts, which Parnell had instigated, and raids on landlords' livestock and fields by the Fenians and the Irish Republican Brotherhood. With torchlight parades and mass meetings in Dublin and other cities, Parnell aroused the populace, declaring that Ireland accept nothing but Home Rule even though it must be under the British Crown.

The Irish people adored him, their tall, handsome, dynamic champion, unafraid of the power of the House of Lords or jealous dissidents in his own Irish Party. The Fenians, that extremely illegal rebel group that struck by night the landlords' properties and tormented the Royal Irish Constabulary, could read between the lines and knew that, though he slightly decried their tactics, he depended on their unceasing aggravation of the authorities to declare Irish unrest.

His strong voice in the crowd, whether calling from a hotel window or standing on a proper platform at a massive rally, inspired patriotism in a land that had suffered brutal oppression for seven hundred years, a people who had never quite surrendered to the rule of Brittania whether in the midst of starvation or war. Charles Stewart Parnell was their hope, their icon, the Uncrowned King of Ireland.

Then the inevitable happened. Within months of the beginning of their cohabitation, Katharine found that she was with child. She had a very special dinner made for him, and they ate together in soft lamplight. Then she told him.

"A child! Our own babe. A part of each of us put together in one tiny package. My Katharine, my own queen, your king is filled with joy!" He kissed her proudly.

Gladstone had him arrested and thrown into Kilmainham Gaol for inciting insurrection with his stubborn demands for Home Rule. His accommodations were not too bad, but he worried about his dearest. He wrote to her: "My own Wifie, I know that you must have been worried by my failure to send you a few words, but my beauty will forgive her own husband. . . ."

As Christmastime neared he wrote from the prison: *"My own darling Queenie, nothing in the world is worth the risk of harm or injury to you. How could I ever live without my own Katie? And if you are in danger, my darling, I will go to you at once."*

A husband's distress at not being with his wifie at this most special time, her pregnancy and their first Christmas. Charles and Katharine had secretly stood together before God and pledged their faithfulness to one another. They felt that they were truly married.

Unbelievably, it was Captain William O'Shea who traveled between Dublin and London discussing the situation with Gladstone, who was looking for a means to settle matters with Parnell without appearing to back down. Apparently, the fact that his wife was committing adultery with his influential friend was not bothering him at that time.

The baby girl was born in February, a delicate little thing. She lay in Katharine's arms on the bed.

"Peg." Katharine's voice was weak but desperate. "I fear for my baby. She doesn't nurse. Her delicate white skin looks almost blue. I wish Charles were here. I cannot bear this alone."

"Let me see what can be done, Mistress," Peg said and hurried out of the room.

When Charles received the note from Peg telling him that his infant child was in danger, he immediately petitioned the warden for furlough from the prison. "I must be released for the funeral of my nephew in Paris," he told him. "I can be back in a week, but it is only proper that I attend with my family."

His sister's son really had died, but Charles went straight to Eltham. Katharine placed his little daughter in his arms.

"My precious babe," he murmured. The great man, the Uncrowned King of Ireland, held his tiny love child, fondled her tiny fingers with his large hand, gazed on the transparent cheeks where dimples appeared like his own true love's. Charles kissed the downy, silken hair on her small head. Then he took Katharine into his arms.

"My dearest one," he whispered. "How can I leave you? If there were any way to stay, I would do it. But I am, after all, a prisoner, and if I don't return in time, I can be sentenced to years more. Let me kiss you and give you strength to deal with whatever comes to pass. Never forget that my heart is with you, my beloved."

Then he left to go back to Kilmainham. Two days later, the infant girl died. With unbelievable gall, Captain William O'Shea begged a day's absence from Parliament "to attend the funeral of *my* baby."

The fact that "they clapped the pride of Erin's Isle into cold Kilmainham Jail" set off a terrible uproar in Ireland. The Irish Party in Commons demanded his release. Negotiations with Parnell came to a standstill in spite of O'Shea's amateurish attempts to make a name for himself by bringing about a deal.

At last, Gladstone himself, the Prime Minister of England, went to the prison in Dublin and made a private arrangement with Charles Parnell. It was called the Kilmainham Treaty. Charles Stewart Parnell was set free and hurried home to his wife after months of separation and tragedy.

Things began to look up for Parnell's efforts to gain Home Rule for Ireland. He and Prime Minister Gladstone were working in agreement for better conditions for the Irish people as a whole. There were special courts and new laws set up. The Land League kept going, sometimes under the leadership of Parnell's sisters, Anna and Fanny, when Michael Davitt found himself arrested and jailed for a time. Gradually, communication between the factions got better. And Charles and Katharine were happy, with another babe on the way.

But then a new chief secretary was sent to administer affairs in Ireland. Young Lord Frederick Cavendish got to Dublin one afternoon and invited Thomas Burke, the under-secretary who was an Irish Catholic, to watch a game of polo. After a good time, the two walked through the dim evening light across Phoenix Park. Suddenly, out of the trees came horsemen riding down on them. Several men jumped off their horses and attacked the two with long knives, leaving them cut to death, lying bleeding on the grass while they rode off.

Who was to blame for this terrible murder? Of course, the Fenians were first blamed. Then it was learned that it wasn't the true Fenians, friends of Charles Parnell, but some radical group calling themselves "The Invincibles" who were impatient of the slow-moving wheels of law and wanted to force Parnell's hand.

At home with Katharine, Charles heard of the horrible crime. "My God," he said to Katharine. "That fine young man and Tom Burke. Neither one guilty of anything except trying to pull together some order in Dublin. I have not condemned much of the mischief that the Fenians do because it helps to emphasize the need to concede to my demands on the English government, but this is monstrous."

"What will you do?" she asked. "You had nothing to do with it."

"One thing I will do. That young Lord Cavendish was Gladstone's own nephew. How awful he must feel, appointing the boy to be chief secretary of Ireland and having him viciously murdered first off. This dreadful thing sickens me. I am going to go straight to William Gladstone and offer to resign my position in

Parliament. It is all that I can do to show my outrage and sympathy for his sorrow and prove that I hate this sort of thing."

But when Parnell faced the prime minister, his resignation was turned down. "I am certain you would not have anything to do with this," Gladstone said. "Such filthy acts are not in your book, I know. We have arrested the killers, a pack of dogs calling themselves 'The Invincibles.' They will be prosecuted. Go on home, Charles, and continue your legal battle for Home Rule. I agree with you on that."

It was an odd life they led. Sure then, Captain O'Shea knew exactly what was going on with Parnell and O'Shea's legal wife. He turned his head and ignored it while sharing his own love nest with Katharine's sister. And it was not beyond him to hint occasionally to Parnell that his fortunes were stumbling somewhat and could use a bit of resuscitation. Parnell quietly paid.

Four years passed, lovely years, while Charles and his Katie had two beautiful, healthy children and lived quietly in Eltham as husband and wife.

Charles Stewart Parnell was almost worshipped by the Irish people. He was indeed revered as "the Uncrowned King." Wherever he went to speak, to converse secretly with Michael Davitt, to meet with Fenian leaders whom he didn't exactly support, but never quite chastised either, the people clung to his wonderful personality, his way with words, his powerful influence in the Parliament, and his undying love and loyalty to his country. His efforts to establish Home Rule were praised and touted everywhere in the green land and not ignored in London by the members of the Irish Party in the House of Commons. Even British society admired and coveted his presence.

Suddenly the British Isles were shaken by an exposé in the *London Times*! A disgruntled and rather unsuccessful journalist named Richard Piggott had sold to the newspaper a letter that apparently was written by Parnell shortly after the Phoenix Park murders. The paper printed it, a handwritten message referring to the terrible deed and commenting in part,

> You should know that to denounce the murders was the only course open to us. . . . I cannot refuse to admit that Burke got no more than his desserts. You are at liberty to show this to others whom you can trust but not let my address be known.

And another letter, which read:

> What are these people waiting for? . . . Our best men are in prison and nothing is being done. Let there be an end to this hesitency. . . . You promised to make it hot for old Forster and Co. Let us have evidence of your power to do so. . . .

A Special Commission was called by the Parliament to investigate the charges that Parnell promoted the murders and bragged about them afterward. Parnell declared that he had never written such evil thoughts. He pointed out that the handwriting was not his, he had not made an *S* like that in years.

Nevertheless, there were those who were opponents of Charles Parnell and his policies for the Irish people, and there were those who suspected him of secret collusion with the Fenians, and there were those who were jealous of his power and popularity. There were those who wanted to believe that he was that underhanded and savage and persistent, he was just too popular.

In the far back of the courtroom gallery, Katharine huddled, praying fervently every minute that somehow Charles' innocence of such criminal support would be proven. He had a good lawyer, Sir Charles Russell, a man who was quite knowledgeable of political factions and the background of Richard Piggott. Russell called Piggott to testify as to the authenticity of the letters he had provided, for a fee, to the *Times*.

After asking Piggott to declare his honesty and belief in the ethics of a court of law, which made the witness extremely nervous, the barrister asked Piggott if he would take a little spelling test. Piggott could see no reason to refuse, he was, after all, a journalist and was certain he had adequate skills in the English language.

Russell called out a few words, simple ones really, and Piggott confidently scribbled his answers on a tablet. Then the lawyer took the tablet and, with a small smile, raised up in his hands the tablet on one side and the copy of the supposed Parnell letter on the other.

"Lords of the Commission, please compare these two writings. You will see that Mr. Piggott in all confidence, misspelled the same word in the test and on his blatant forgery of a letter! The word *hesitancy* has been spelled h-e-s-i-t-e-n-c-y in both documents, proving that the same hand wrote them both!"

Piggott fell apart. His answers to subsequent questions were erratic, confused, contradicting one another. The Special Commission threw out the charges. It was over. Parnell was cleared and his supporters celebrated!

All of Ireland and the Irish Party heaved a sigh of relief. Parnell could go on stronger than ever in his battle for his people.

But more trouble was headed the way of Charles and Katharine. Willie O'Shea became restless. Aunt Ben couldn't possibly live much longer. What if Mrs. Benjamin learned of Katharine's covert adultery? Would the old lady cut her out of her will altogether? When she died, could someone challenge William's right to Katharine's inheritance? After all, he had not lived with her for years. Perhaps it was time to make an appearance, for the record, as a devoted husband.

He began to be a nuisance. When he chose to come home to his wife Katharine, there was nothing she nor Charles could do. He would arrive as if it were quite normal for him to drop in, sit by the fire, take his supper, and go to bed (in his own suite, of course).

Charles and Katie moved away from Eltham. "Mr. and Mrs. Fox" rented a cottage on the southern coast of England. Willie O'Shea followed them. "Mr. Preston" found a home for his family in another seacoast town. O'Shea calmly came home. Finally, in Brighton, Mrs. O'Shea rented a large house for her husband and children.

One evening, after the children were in bed, Charles and Katharine were settled down in their suite upstairs, resting by an open window in the cool night air. Charles had donned his dressing gown over his nightshirt and Katharine was just getting ready to let her rich auburn hair down from its pins and combs. There was a loud rapping on the front door.

Katharine hurried to open the bedroom door a crack to see who was disturbing their quiet evening. She was not too surprised to hear Peg say loudly, "Why, Captain O'Shea, Mrs. Katie was not expecting you this evening!"

"Well now, Peg, I had a little holiday from Parliament and decided to come home and spend some time with my wife." Boldly, Willie O'Shea marched into his house and handed the maid his cloak and hat and cane. "Where will I find my darling?"

Peg, startled, stammered uncertainly in response.

Katharine turned to tell Charles what was happening. His chair by the open window was empty.

Captain O'Shea demanded a bit of supper, and Peg ordered the curious cook to prepare the meal without any questions. Katharine came downstairs and had a cup of tea, her own dinner long past.

When his supper was over, Willie retired to the drawing room, insisting that Katharine join him there. Looking around, he commented, "You have lovely taste, my dear. You have chosen very attractive furnishings for *our* little home."

"You can stop that nonsense right now, Willie O'Shea," she ordered in a low, angry voice. "It was not your money that provided these things, and this is not your home. What are you trying to do with all this cozy, family talk?"

"Just trying to draw my wife back to my side after all

your wanderings." His voice was sarcastic and amused.

"If I had had a true husband, there would never have been wanderings," Kitty hissed. "You were so busy 'wandering' with my sister, you seemed not to notice that your 'wife' was making a life with someone who truly loved her, supported her, and met her needs whether they were material or affectionate."

"But, my dear, the world needs to see us together, to recognize that we are legally man and wife and living in our own home."

"You mean that Aunt Ben must see us together, don't you? I hope she lives to be one hundred and you starve to death waiting for her to die!"

Once more, the knocker on the front door sounded. Peg shook her head. Who else would be coming on this strange evening? What more confusion would it bring? She marched across the hall to open the door on who knew what more strange goings on. The spectacle that met her eyes left her mouth open in speechless shock.

Charles Stewart Parnell stood on the doorstep. He was dressed in an outrageous assortment of sporting attire. On his head, he wore a heavy, brown fur cap fit for a trip to the Artic to hunt polar bear. Over a coarse, tweed hunting jacket with many pockets for ammunition, he had put on a bright scarlet knitted vest. But hunting wild animals was obviously not his total aspiration for his ensemble was completed with a pair of tall, black wading boots rising all the way up to his hips.

Captain O'Shea came into the hall when he heard the involuntary exclamation that came from Peg's mouth. Willie's pale blue eyes went round at the incredible sight.

"Been out fishing for eels," Parnell said cheerfully. "I thought that, as long as I was in Brighton, I would come to call. Perhaps you can put me up for the night?"

Willie O'Shea stood in the hall dumbfounded, unable to find words to cover the situation. The lie was so unspeakably blatant. That unspeakably ridiculous mix of clothes was clearly borrowed out of desperate necessity.

Behind Willie, Katharine's eyes sparkled with merriment. It was all she could do to keep her hand over her mouth to smother the hysterical laughter that shook her body. Who but Charles would have the incredible gall to beg some clothes from lord knows who and come asking for lodging in his own house? The colossal brazenness of the man! *How she loved him!*

Willie mumbled something with confused hospitality and, after a polite cup of tea, the trio stumbled up the stairs, to bed down in three separate chambers. The next morning, Charles appeared at breakfast dressed in his frock coat and striped trousers. No one asked him where he got them.

Finally Aunt Ben died. Immediately Katharine's family challenged the will. A subtle understanding had been made that, out of the inheritance, Katharine would pay O'Shea twenty thousand pounds to arrange quietly a bill of divorcement and go his way, allowing her and Parnell to just as quietly make their alliance legal. With court manipulations regarding the will going on, there was no money to buy him off.

O'Shea was furious. He filed for divorce, shouting to all that his wife had been living in sin with the great Charles Stewart Parnell for many years. The *London*

Times, having been made a fool over the Phoenix Park matter, was delighted to take hold of the story.

Catholic Ireland rocked with shock and dismay. Their beloved champion, their Uncrowned King, involved in such ugliness, was a fornicating wife-stealer. Victorian England was equally as stunned. In spite of his dogged efforts to bring Home Rule to Ireland, he had commanded great respect in that country. Now they clucked their tongues and shook their heads.

Parliament was mildly surprised. Most of them were quite aware of the situation but, if Captain William O'Shea did not care, why should they bother about it? However, they could forget about the Home Rule. No one would align himself in a vote with the shame of Parnell.

The world came crashing down around the loving pair. Music Hall comedians found in it a plethora of material to make jokes. Katherine's family turned their backs on them in disgrace, happy to be able to use the scandal in their own suit against Katharine, ignoring the indiscretions of her sister.

Katharine and Charles kept out of the public eye and tried to protect the children from it all. When the divorce came to court, they did not appear. In so doing, they set the pitied, abused husband free to bring all manner of unchallenged charges against them. But the witness that topped off the plaintiff's case was Peg.

The poor lady's maid was forced by her ethics to answer the command to appear in court. O'Shea's attorney pounded pointed questions at her and, because she was a religious and honest woman, she could not lie. In tears, she verified the unbelievable story of O'Shea's visit to Brighton, and Parnell's disappearance and then outrageous appearance at the door as if making a spontaneous call on the family.

O'Shea got his divorce. Parnell's enemies crowed. Katharine's family sat back, satisfied that the inheritance was theirs. Charles and Katharine were quietly and legally married in a private ceremony. The Irish Party called a special meeting to decide what to do with their erstwhile wonderful leader.

The meeting of the Party was a disaster of protocol. Emotions ran amuck. There was fear that without Parnell, the strength of the Irish Party in Parliament would wither away to nothing. And yet, with Parnell, and his disgrace in place, the members would come crawling into their seats, embarrassed and worthless. Charles Parnell sat quietly, not defending himself, only hoping that his past performance for their goals would speak for itself.

Someone rose up and began to try to calm and clarify the purpose of the gathering. "Gentlemen," he shouted. "Remember our purpose here today is simply to determine who will be the Master of the Party!"

A sarcastic voice came sharp and clear from the back of the assembly, "Perhaps we should be considering who will be the 'Mistress' of the Party!"

A great hullabaloo rose. Some members were slightly amused, some angry, and some afraid of the offense to Parnell. A member called out, "I appeal to the chairman to call for order!"

Parnell stood up, white with fury, and looked into the crowd of almost hysterical MPs. "It would be better if you appeal to that cowardly little scoundrel who dares in an assembly of Irishmen to insult a woman!"

It was a while before the meeting ended with a decision. Charles Stewart Parnell was ousted from the position of Head of the Irish Party in the Parliament in London.

When he reached their house in Walsingham Terrace, Katharine met him at the door. "My dear Charles, I have never seen you look so weary. I need not ask how the meeting went. I have a little friend who is the wife of another MP and she has told me how you defended me before those vultures. Know this, my dear and faithful husband, I have never loved you more than I do at this moment."

～のく

They were married in 1890. Parnell tried desperately to continue his work for his beloved country but too much distress affected him, and his health began to fail with alarming swiftness. After a final speaking trip from London to his homeland in a cold and rainy September in 1891, he barely made it home in time to die in the arms of the woman he loved enough to risk his reputation in the church, political success, and all he had in the world for his "own darling Queen."

Maud Gonne and the Poet Yeats

She was breathtakingly beautiful. The roles she played on the stages of Dublin at the turn of the twentieth century were stunning. William Butler Yeats adored her. But she was not satisfied.

In the heart of the young actress was a constant agitation to see Ireland free of British rule.

On the stage, the old woman raised her head a bit. "I have hope of getting my beautiful fields back again, the hope of putting the strangers out of my house."

The family represented in the play gently told her that those who wanted to help her would surely fail. "I am not afraid. If they are put down today, they will get the upper hand tomorrow!"

The crowd in St. Theresa's Hall in Dublin roared with approval. The analogy was so clear. The old woman was Shan Van Vocht, beleaguered and despairing Ireland. Throughout the scenes in the play the audience became more and more fired with patriotic fervor.

Lastly, the old woman left the stage by a door in the set, and soon another person came through that door, a man. One of the characters asked, "Did you see an old woman going down the path?"

"I did not," he answered, "but I saw a young girl and she had the walk of a queen!"

The audience went wild. Shouts of "Erin go Bragh!" "Out with the English!"

"Freedom for Ireland!" rang through the hall.

Behind the curtain the old woman straightened up and became the magnificent and beautiful Maud Gonne, the most celebrated and beloved actress in Ireland.

"Willy!" she cried. "Willy, you did it! *Cathleen ni Houlihan* is a success and more! It has inspired zeal. Sure, the revolution is underway!"

She pulled off the heavy gray wig, letting her shining, golden brown tresses fall around her shoulders as she headed back to the stage for many curtain calls.

At last the audience filtered out of the hall, still praising the play and the great lady who performed. Maud took the hand of William Butler Yeats and drew him with her toward the dressing room.

Once there, she stepped behind a screen, tearing off the ragged shawl and gown, exulting at the results of their work. Yeats leaned against the wall, adjusting his large, round glasses and running his fingers through his tousled, dark hair.

"I'm so glad it served its purpose, Maud dear. If my pitiful efforts can strike such passion, then I am delighted. I hope our compatriots in the Irish Republican

Brotherhood will be pleased, also. Now, my love, wipe off your wrinkles. I must ask you a question."

She laughed, in clear, tinkling bell sounds. "Oh, Willy. *Not again.*"

"Yes, my Maudie. I will ask again and again. I will not stop until you say you will marry me."

"William Butler Yeats, you know I love you, but it is not the kind of love that marries. What would you do with a wife like me, and yourself so gentle and bookish? I would drive you to distraction. How could you abide a wife who marches down the street with Countess Markievicz bearing anti-British banners? You would be so ashamed of me if I wind up in prison again. And you would be out of your mind with worry every time I drove into the Liberties with a wagon load of food and blankets for the poor! No, my sweet Willy, I will never marry you. It would be the ruin of your poetry, and I will not destroy the beautiful soul of my dearest friend. The world would not forgive me for that."

"Maud, I will wait for you forever. We were meant to be wed. We are alike, you and I."

Maud came out from behind the screen dressed in a lovely, dark blue gown. Picking up a wide-brimmed hat with feathers, she leaned over the mirror to pin it into place. "I'm afraid I coerced you into joining the IRB with me. It's a rebel I am and always will be. Willy, my dear one, it would be cruel to pull you away from the wonderful words you write, grand words that bless the people who read them.

"As for me, I must fight against the unspeakable op-pression of England that we have suffered for seven hundred years, the outrageous laws and starvation foisted on the Irish people. Ireland is a tired old woman, sure, but I am not and I will never give in."

As Willy and Maud slipped out the stage door, they could hear the milling crowd in front of the theatre, still raising their voices with patriotic slogans and fervor.

"I wonder at the influence of my simple words, the fire they have kindled in men's hearts," William murmured.

"You only fanned the flame that has been smoldering for centuries and of late has begun to glow brighter. Now you must return to your first love, poetry."

"Not for a while," he said as they walked along the dark, cobbled street. "This success will only reassure Lady Augusta Gregory that I am the one to go to America to lecture on the theatre and raise interest in the Abbey Theatre. She is scheduling a tour of eight months."

"Willy, no! William, the theatre is not your life. Poetry is yours. I love you and I feel that I have inspired you to write. It is as if your wonderful verses are our children, the only ones we will ever have. Your words are sensitive to beauty and to sorrows. Why must you waste your time promoting the theatre company? Augusta Gregory is using your popularity in her efforts to establish a theatre in Dublin!"

"It is for the people of Ireland, don't you see, love? I concur with Augusta that the people of Ireland will find themselves lifted up when they have the finest of the arts at their will. Irish writers have proven themselves to the world. The Irish people need to recognize the greatness in their blood. I have spent many a day at her home in Coole Park with Synge and O'Casey and Shaw and Masefield and even my brother, Jack, all of us as feverish to excite the good minds of the Irish as you are to rid us from the demeaning English. So, I will go. Forty weeks is not forever. *Cathleen ni Houlihan* will keep you busy until I come back to once more beg you to marry me."

Maud stopped under a lamppost. She took the man's face in her hands and studied the narrow jaw line, the deep brown eyes, the shock of hair that never wanted to lie in place, the lips that always seemed to pout a bit.

"My dear, dear, Willy. You are precious to me. Go to America if you must. You have your crusade and I have mine."

When he left her at her apartment near Trinity College, she climbed the stairs with light feet. The thrill of success was still vibrating in her, making her full of joy. Too bad dear old Willy was so determined to marry her. It hurt her to continually reject his proposals, for she did indeed have a love for him, but there was no way she would pull him any more into the simmering rebellion of the IRB. As his brother, Jack, and his father were artists with paint and brush, William Butler Yeats was an artist with words, speaking the innermost senses of the people in words so perfect and beautiful that they took your breath. He loved the mystic of Ireland, the faery folk and the spirits in the mists of the mountains and the ghosts of ancient legends. The work of the Irish Republican Brotherhood and those who fought England's iron hand in Ireland was hard as the stones of the Burren—and sometimes bloody.

She had first met the gentle poet when she delivered

a letter to his father from "Pagan" John O'Leary, the grand old leftover Fenian from the rebellions in the 1850s. Immediately the very tall, beautiful, and rambunctious revolutionary actress and the quiet, thoughtful, and dreamy writer were attracted to each other. So she invited him to her apartment with the others.

It was a strange assortment of characters that slipped into the Georgian rooming house on those late nights. O'Leary himself was there, his bright eyes and long, white beard reflecting the firelight as he drank his tea, and his inspiring, angry, inflammatory words filling the room. Around him, clustered on whatever seat or space of floor they could find, were men thirsty to hear him confirm their own ideals, Arthur Griffith, Douglas Hyde, William and Jack Yeats, and several other young, brilliant minds. Pagan John set fire to their determination that Ireland could someday be a totally free nation. It was possible! Those were grand times they shared in the firelit darkness, hidden from the ears of British informers.

It wasn't long, though, that Maud came out into the open with her opinions. The National League sent her to Donegal, where massive numbers of evictions were going on. In spite of the land reforms passed by the Gladstone administration, hundreds of farmers were being tossed out of their tiny, stone cottages to make space for the more profitable cattle ranches of the landlords.

She was outraged. Whole families whose ancestors had lived on those infinitesimal plots of earth were dragged out into the roads, the houses knocked down before their eyes, and driven into the countryside with not a hope of shelter. Maud was compelled to stand and watch the peelers and land agents drag out an old grandmother, too ill to move off her mattress, and dump her on the ground while her daughter and little grandchildren wailed helplessly.

The tall, fiery young woman began to find bog areas, which were barely useable, and helped the evicted people to build little huts of wattle for shelter. Protests were organized among the people. Maud Gonne fired letter after letter to the newspapers describing the greedy actions of English landlords in the hinterlands of Donegal.

She was threatened with arrest for being a rabble-rouser. Finally she had to go back to Dublin.

There came a time when all of England was celebrating the sixtieth anniversary of Queen Victoria's reign. Maud found William Yeats at his home in Sligo.

"Willy, we've come up with the grandest plan! The old Famine Queen is celebrating sixty years of her imperialist aggression. You must come to Dublin. We are going to have a march right through the city. The nationalists are going to carry a coffin with a sign hung on it that reads, "The British Empire." And Arthur has dug up the statistics, so placards will display the number of Irish people who have starved to death and been evicted from their little farms and how many have been hung for political reasons during her time. Oh, the RIC and the peelers are not going to like it!" Maud smiled gleefully.

Yeats frowned. "Maud, I hope you don't plan to be one of the marchers. Yes, of course you will. I know better than to try to talk you out of it. Well then, I might as well get into it, too."

"Wonderful! I was sure you would. The Royal Irish Constabulary won't dare to arrest you, the people love you too much."

The day came, June 22, 1897. Masses of marchers filled the Dublin streets, led by nationalist leaders. Maud Gonne and William Butler Yeats led the parade.

Indeed, the British authorities were not pleased. As the crowd neared the Lord Nelson pylon, the RIC and English soldiers burst from side streets, wielding clubs and rifles.

"Maud, here they are! I have to get you out of here!" Yeats shouted.

"Not I! I stand right here!"

Shoving people, cracking heads with rifle butts, knocking down and trampling whole groups of marchers with their heavy boots, the soldiers and police broke into the parade. It became a riot in the streets! Maud braced herself and fought back, kicking and scratching every Anglo face she could reach. At her height of over six feet, she reached many before an officer finally brought her to the ground with his rifle.

Willy struggled to pull her across the pavement through the flailing arms and legs of the crowd and into a doorway. He leaned over her, wiping away blood and dirt with his silk handkerchief.

"Dear God, Maud, are you going to live? How badly are you hurt?"

"Live?" Maud exulted. "Willy, *this is living!* This is Ireland coming to life. The more they try to hurt and kill and jail the Irish, the more fury they bring upon themselves. Glory!"

The fighting went on into the dark night. By the light of the lamps on Ha'penny Bridge, Yeats gazed with astonishment on the face of Maud Gonne, Ireland's favorite actress. Her eyes shone with exuberance, her smile was strong and proud. She radiated *joy!*

"It was so grand, Willy. Our people are seeing just how far the English will go to hold us under their heel. Just wait until next year. Then we will commemorate the Rising of 1798. The Anglos will not like that, either!"

They didn't like it. But the agitation went on. Newspaper stories, protests, mass rallies. Maud spoke sometimes to twenty thousand or more people, shouting truths about the horrors of Irish native life, the cruelty, the starvation and death. And the British authorities watched her closely.

In 1899, the English, not satisfied that "the sun never set on the British Empire," attacked a little country in South Africa and attempted to take over the Boers, the Dutch settlers there. The Irish nationals were incensed. The Boers fought for their lives with guerrilla warfare.

Victoria's war was not going well. The English army became depleted. So, Her Majesty, old as she was, took herself to Ireland trying to entice the enlistment of young Irishmen into the British army. So, the old queen rode through the streets of Dublin.

On one side of Phoenix Park, Victoria stood on the grass and handed candy treats to little children. Some five thousand youngsters came.

On the opposite side of the huge park, Maud Gonne, the actress, was surrounded by thirty thousand children and treated them to candies.

Victoria's public relations didn't work. The Irish saw in the brutal invasion of the small country a similarity to their own history. Maud Gonne and William Yeats lent their voices to the cry against the Boer War. Not one Irishman enlisted in the British army. However, an Irish Brigade made up of volunteers made their way to Africa and fought side by side with the Boers. One of those volunteers was Major John MacBride.

While Yeats was touring and speaking to his many admirers in America in support of the Abbey Theatre, Maud continued her lifestyle. She went with the Daughters of Erin to ease the suffering of the poor, of which there were many both inside and outside of Dublin. She made speeches at rallies of nationalists in parks and halls, anywhere she could be heard, and generally annoyed the British authorities. And the crowds at St. Theresa's Hall were steadily attracted by her magnificent beauty and inspired to a patriotic frenzy by *Cathleen ni Houlihan.*

It was while lending her popular presence to a rally in Phoenix Park that Maud was introduced to a newly assimilated member of the Brotherhood, Major John MacBride. The major was just back from commanding the Irish Brigade in the Boer Wars. He wore a hearty black mustache on his African-suntanned face. There was a spark of humor in his china blue eyes and the brass buttons on his uniform shone like crowns. Maud liked him. She found herself fascinated by the tales of his exploits in the Boer War, even though the major made sure his own adventures were quite heroic.

As the rally wound down, the major sought her out. "Could I be asking the great and wonderful Maud

Gonne to share a cup of tea with me?"

She didn't deny his description of her, and she happily agreed to take tea with him at The Clarence. Sitting in the hotel dining room, they found themselves engrossed in the IRB efforts to gain independence for Ireland. Yeats' gentle assurances that he agreed with Maud's wild nationalist dreams faded out of sight compared to the brilliant spark of military ingenuity and fiery determination of Major MacBride.

"You intrigue me," she told him. "Have you always been a patriot?"

"I'm afraid I have." A white smile flashed across his face. "I was raised with the military by an Irish father. He taught me that the best way to overcome the British control was to become a better soldier than they and beat them at their own game. That I have done. I think the time has come to lend my skills to the effort for freedom in Ireland, so here I am."

Maud was thrilled. Here was a fine man with military abilities ready to fight a revolution if necessary. He was in full harmony with her ideals and motives. How grand!

She laughed. "You have one more advantage than I, Major. My father was an English officer and my mother Irish, both very proper and loyal to the Crown. I remember how I disgraced my father when I was only nineteen, already on fire for freedom in Ireland.

"They took me to a ball at the residence of the viceroy in Dublin Castle. The Prince of Wales was there, Prince Edward Albert. He seemed to be rather taken with me, and he asked me if I could sing. I told him I could, so he escorted me to the platform and very honorably presented me to the crowd. I sang. I gave my voice all my power. It was 'The Wearin' o' the Green!' I sang:

> *How's poor old Ireland and how does she stand?*
> *She's the most distressful country that ever yet*
> > *was seen,*
> *For they're hanging men and women there for the*
> > *wearin'o' the green.*
> *And if the color we must wear is England's*
> > *cruel red,*
> *Let it remind us of the blood that Ireland has shed.*

"My father was horrified." She grinned with delight. "And, sure, I'll never forget the look on His Royal Highness, the prince's face! So you see, I have shamed my family with my patriotic enthusiasm."

A hearty laugh burst from Major MacBride in the quiet dining room, which caused many eyes to look his way. He lowered his voice but he was delighted by her story. They continued to talk for hours, relishing their common interest. By the time he took her home in a hansom cab, she was thoroughly captivated.

That was the first of many rendezvous. By the time Yeats got back from America, Maud and the major were married.

Willy was crushed. His poetry changed. The lofty dreams of love and perfection gave way to just a bit of bitterness, just a bit, for it was not in his gentle soul to be ugly. Maud was sorry to see it. But slowly, over some years, his work regained and even surpassed its greatness. He vowed he would never marry.

In due time, Maud presented the major with a son, Sean. But the major had another love affair with a powerful rival, Irish whiskey. He became abusive, cruel. Maud divorced him and left for France to raise her son.

It was more than ten years before she came back to Ireland. It was after the Easter Rising of 1916.

"Willy, what has happened here?" she asked Yeats as they sat at dinner in her new flat. "Every major building in Dublin has been nearly destroyed! Piles of stone and debris where fine public buildings used to be. And I found that John MacBride among many fine friends of ours was executed without trial."

"Poor Maud, you must have been so involved with the World War in Europe that you haven't heard the whole story. Padraig Pearse and several others of our nationalist group declared Ireland to be a free nation by making a speech on the steps of the General Post Office. They were prepared to start a revolution then and there, and they had the Irish Republican Army positioned in vital spots all over the city. Of course, they lost the battle, but it took the English a week to make them surrender, what with British gunboats firing at them from the Liffey and RIC and peelers along with British army troops surrounding them. You would have been proud of them all, Maudie."

"But they *shot* them! They surrendered, and they shot them!"

"True, but in doing so, the English authorities infuriated the people. Actually, most of Dublin thought at first that the rebels were engaged in terrible foolishness, Pearse and Plunkett and the lot of them making trouble. But when they were so viciously shot in Kilmainham

Gaol yard, most of the people have become anti-Anglo. The English have made one grand mistake."

Sadness to the point of weeping tugged at the poet's lips. "I mourn for those men who used to sit around your fire and listen to Pagan O'Leary and now have given their lives. But the irony of it all has made them heroes, and well they should be."

"My heart breaks for them, Willy. I have never wanted to see them die for the freedom I keep harping about. I rather wish I had never made speeches and stirred up the people."

"I have had the same reflections. If I had seen ahead, would I have used my words and my voice to encourage them? I truly don't know," Yeats mused. "A revolution was in full swing. A big, handsome fellow named Michael Collins, a relentless warrior, and one Eamon DeValera, an Irish American, picked up the torch. The IRA tormented and struck at the English any way and every way. Lives have been lost on both sides. The old hope of Home Rule for Ireland—that was passed in Parliament but somehow slipped their minds to implement—is not going to satisfy the people now. This time, they are demanding a full and complete break from England!"

"Wonderful. That has been my hope all along!"

"It would be grand indeed if it came about, Maud, but I fear our country has gone mad. Michael Collins, wonderful warrior but no diplomat he, was sent to England with two other good representatives of the IRA to make a treaty with the Crown. He came back with a pitiable contract they call 'The Irish Free State.' The country has its own little government, but still we must swear allegiance to the king of England. England may draft young Irishmen to fight their battles in foreign lands. England controls our harbors and commerce. True freedom is as far away as ever. I intend to run for the Free State Senate in order to try to instill some sort of sense in their movement. But the disagreement between the two concepts has become a civil war, Irish patriots fighting Irish patriots. Maud, our people are treating one another more viciously than they fought the British, believing that they must obey the interim government or continue to hold out for full freedom, either one being traitors."

Immediately, Maud was on her feet. "I don't blame anyone for refusing to accept such a devious scheme, just a *name* to placate our rebels. It won't do, Willy. I must do something!"

"Maud, please do not go out to incite more zeal. There is enough of that. It keeps the interim government busy cramming more and more anti-Treaty prisoners into our old jails. If you must lead a crusade, have pity on those who are imprisoned. The conditions are deplorable. Mountjoy prison is bad enough but they have reopened Kilmainham Gaol, that broken-down old edifice, and men and women are being kept in filth and disease-ridden, cold wards."

"I believe you are right, Willy dear. You must go on with your wonderful writing of beautiful poetry to lift folk out of the horrors of war, and I will give my energy to easing pain—if I can. How is your new little wife? I believe her name is 'George'? An unusual name."

"Not especially unusual these days, Maud. Georgie is a bit odd, if you would call it that. She is deeply interested in the occult and mysticism, as you know I have always been. We are a match. I still adore you, my majestic, fervent heroine, but true it is that we would have exhausted one another."

Maud was not in Ireland long before she learned that every word Yeats told her about her beloved land was true. Destruction and war were everywhere. The newspapers reported too many atrocities happening all over the island, good people believing themselves to be in the right killing other good people who disagreed. Children at play carried wooden weapons mimicking the soldiers who were constantly in view. It was a time of confusion, turbulence, and great, great fear.

Maud Gonne MacBride called upon women she knew to protest the prison conditions, the putrid food, the cold wind swirling through broken windows, one toilet to serve 130 prisoners, the brutal treatment of the guards to inmates, men and women alike.

Maud's troops of women were glad to go out onto O'Connell Street every Sunday afternoon, marching, carrying signs, singing patriotic songs in defiance of the government. The soldiers chased them away, but they kept coming back, calling attention to the inhuman treatment of Irish people in jails.

More than one hundred joined the Women's Prisoners Defense League. They were glad to go, women like Mary MacSwiney whose brother had died from a hunger strike in prison, and Nora Connolly whose father, James, was one of the fourteen executed by firing squad in Kilmainham after the Easter Rising, and Grace Plunkett, married to Joseph Plunkett only five hours before he also was shot in the prison exercise yard, and Margaret Pearse, mother of Padraig and Willie Pearse, the poetic dreamers who led the insurrection and were also shot in Kilmainham. Kathleen Clarke was one of the women, she who not only lost her husband, Thomas Clarke, to the unlawful executions, but her brother Edward Daly also, and saw her mother beaten to death with the rifle butts of the Black and Tans, the mob of convicted criminals let loose from British prisons to beat down the Irish.

Oh, the women were glad to band together to protest government alliance with the British. Maud's ex-husband, the father of her son, Sean, had faced down the barrels of the firing squad with that group. The Countess Constance Markievicz, the Irish girl who had married a Polish count and came back to Ireland to become a militant leader of the Easter Rising, barely escaped being executed for her leadership in the 1916 rebellion. She gave her considerable support to the women's organization.

Throughout the week, the women spent their days outside prison gates, passing messages to those inside the cold walls, along with a bit of food or a warm scrap of wool when the guards allowed. Sometimes they stood in a crowd below the high walls, shouting encouragement to the faces that appeared at the barred windows above. Often, as they sat by the gates, they "sewed seams of bitterness" toward the turn-coat governing body that tried to beat down rebellion against anti-Treaty forces. And then on Sundays, back they went to the streets of Dublin, Maud Gonne and the Countess leading the rally.

The army came out against them with firehoses and

rubber bullets. The women came back. One Sunday the soldiers shot real bullets, coming close to killing some of the marchers.

Finally, by government decree, the women were rounded up, and Maud found herself 1 of 150 women crushed into the already overcrowded cells of Kilmainham Gaol.

Coming into the building off the streets, they needed to be body-searched to be sure they brought no weapons. The younger girls were searched with much more enthusiasm than necessary by half-drunken guards, and the young ladies came through with clothing ripped nearly off their bodies. The older women, who objected, had their fingers pounded by clubs as they clung to the bars, and some were thrown down the tall, narrow iron staircases of Kilmainham.

Countess Markievicz was assigned kitchen duty, trying to clean the large tin cans that served as dishes for the unspeakable pottage that was their meal. The cans were old and rusty inside, and most of the time the washers had no soap or soda to use.

On occasion, they were pushed outside into the exercise yard. Nora Connolly, Grace Plunkett, Kathleen Clarke, and Margaret Pearse laid their hands and heads against the bullet-pitted wall and wept, believing they could still see the blood stains of their loved ones.

Then the word came that the entire crowd of soiled, sickened, cold, and bloody women were to be transferred to an old workhouse outside of Dublin. The guards came to round them up.

Maud pulled herself to her feet. "I know that place. If you can believe it, that ancient building is worse than this, full of disease and rats. We will not go. As political prisoners, we refuse!"

As one voice the women shouted, "We will not go!"

Then the guards came at them with clubs.

"Hunger strike!" The word went up and was shouted over and over in spite of blows to their heads and faces.

For twenty days, they lay curled up together on the floor. When the rancid pottage was brought to them, they poured it on the floor or out the windows. Kicks, fists, pulled hair did not break their resolve.

Then one day, a guard came looking for Maud Gonne. "There's a senator outside wanting you," he said, dragging her to her feet. "Says he's going to take you out of here."

She yanked back with what strength she could muster and dropped back to the floor. "I'll not go, not unless we all go!"

Hunger-hoarse voices began a chorus. "Go, Maudie! Please go! If you are outside, you can tell the newspapers and the people the truth about the prisons, just as we tried to do with our demonstrations. If you go, we will try to eat that swill and watch for you to get us free!"

Maud looked around the room at the white, shriveled faces. "I'll go," she whispered.

Senator William Butler Yeats stood waiting in the hall to receive Maud as the guard dragged her through the doorway.

"My God, Maud, you are nearly dead!" His brown eyes grew wide with horror behind his glasses. "Here, you guard. Don't drag her like that! Pick her up and carry her to my auto. She is a lady, a fine lady. You will treat her as such!"

Yeats wrapped Maud's cold, nearly lifeless body in a warm fur lap robe and laid her head on his shoulder while they were driven through the streets of Dublin. "I am taking you home. Georgie will see to it that you are well treated until you can get your health back. Your son, Sean, is there waiting for you. That young man is ready to take on the whole British army for you, and I believe someday he will."

Willy Yeats tucked the robe tenderly close around the gaunt shoulders of the woman he had so passionately loved and who still held a place in his heart.

"Maud, why will you do things like this?" he scolded gently. "The battling is just about over. The IRA is giving up, and the civil war may soon be a memory."

"Never!" she whispered urgently. "Never, Willy. I don't want to see murders and people suffering, but someday the centuries of horrible oppression will be over and our green land will be truly free to prosper and thrive as Ireland was always meant to do!"

Yeats shook his head sadly and murmured,

"Did that play of mine send out
Certain men the English shot?"

~⊙~

Maud Gonne MacBride lived to see her dream for Ireland come true. In 1949, after years of negotiations and demands, the last strings of control were taken away from the British, and The Republic of Ireland, the twenty-six southern counties, was set free to expand and prosper and become the happy, flourishing nation it is today.

Epilogue

In her inaugural address in 1990, the first woman president of Ireland, the lovely Mary Robinson, stated, "As a woman, I want women who have felt themselves outside history to be written back into history."

Look again.

Index

About the Illustrator

Michael Allen Lowe is a graduate of the Kansas City Art Institute. He is the owner of 10/10 Fine Art Gallery in Kansas City, MO.

You may contact him at: ArtStudio702@aol.com.